Neuropsycho

MW00652798

Georg Northoff presents the first introduction to neuropsychoanalysis and the search for a brain-based understanding and explanation of our psyche and its psychodynamic features.

This book covers the key features of psychodynamics, including the concepts of self, narcissism, defense mechanisms, unconsciousness/ consciousness, attachment and trauma, energy/cathexis, and depression/ schizophrenia. After reviewing past and current state-of-the-art models and their limitations, Northoff uniquely links these psychodynamic features to temporal and spatial features in the brain (and body). The key element in connecting brain and mind is dynamic, the pattern of change over time: from brain dynamic to psychodynamic – dynamic is thus shared by brain and psyche as their "common currency". This spatiotemporal approach offers novel and sometimes surprising insights into the elusive connection of brain and mind. Ultimately, this carries important clinico-therapeutic implications for psychodynamic psychotherapy in a spatiotemporal sense, such as through spatiotemporal psychotherapy.

This accessible volume will be of great interest to neuroscientists, neuropsychoanalysts, psychologists, psychoanalysts, and anyone interested in the brain–mind connection. Additional material for the present book including figures and tables as well as short talks about each chapter can be found on this website (www.georgnorthoff.com) including the author's YouTube channel.

Georg Northoff is a philosopher, psychiatrist, and neuroscientist at the University of Ottawa, Canada, holding a Canada Research Chair for Mind, Brain Imaging and Neuroethics. His research focuses on the brain–mind connection and its subjectivity; he has published numerous books and papers on his unique spatiotemporal approach. His website is www.georgnorthoff.com.

Routledge Introductions to Contemporary Psychoanalysis

Series Editor
Aner Govrin, Ph.D.
Executive Editor
Tair Caspi, Ph.D.
Assistant Editor
Yael Peri Herzovich

"Routledge Introductions to Contemporary Psychoanalysis" is one of the prominent psychoanalytic publishing ventures of our day. It will comprise dozens of books that will serve as concise introductions dedicated to influential concepts, theories, leading figures, and techniques in psychoanalysis covering every important aspect of psychoanalysis.

The length of each book is fixed at 40,000 words.

The series' books are designed to be easily accessible to provide informative answers in various areas of psychoanalytic thought. Each book will provide updated ideas on topics relevant to contemporary psychoanalysis – from the unconscious and dreams, projective identification and eating disorders, through neuropsychoanalysis, colonialism, and spiritual-sensitive psychoanalysis. Books will also be dedicated to prominent figures in the field, such as Melanie Klein, Jaque Lacan, Sandor Ferenczi, Otto Kernberg, and Michael Eigen.

Not serving solely as an introduction for beginners, the purpose of the series is to offer compendiums of information on particular topics within different psychoanalytic schools. We ask authors to review a topic but also address the readers with their own personal views and contribution to the specific chosen field. Books will make intricate ideas comprehensible without compromising their complexity.

We aim to make contemporary psychoanalysis more accessible to both clinicians and the general educated public.

Aner Govrin – Editor

Neuropsychoanalysis
A Contemporary Introduction
Georg Northoff

For more information about this series, please visit: www.routledge.com

Neuropsychoanalysis

A Contemporary Introduction

Georg Northoff

Routledge
Taylor & Francis Group

LONDON AND NEW YORK

Designed cover image: © Michal Heiman, Asylum 1855–2020,
The Sleeper (video, psychoanalytic sofa and Plate 34), exhibition
view, Herzliya Museum of Contemporary Art, 2017

First published 2023
by Routledge
4 Park Square, Milton Park, Abingdon, Oxon OX14 4RN

and by Routledge
605 Third Avenue, New York, NY 10158

Routledge is an imprint of the Taylor & Francis Group, an informa business

© 2023 Georg Northoff

British Library Cataloguing-in-Publication Data
A catalogue record for this book is available from the
British Library

Library of Congress Cataloging-in-Publication Data
Names: Northoff, Georg, author.
Title: Neuropsychoanalysis : a contemporary introduction /
  Georg Northoff.
Description: Abingdon, Oxon ; New York, NY : Routledge, 2023. |
  Series: Routledge introductions to contemporary psychoanalysis |
  Includes bibliographical references and index.
Identifiers: LCCN 2022038693 (print) | LCCN 2022038694
  (ebook) | ISBN 9780367678074 (paperback) | ISBN
  9780367678043 (hardback) | ISBN 9781003132905 (ebook)
Subjects: LCSH: Psychoanalysis. | Neuropsychiatry. |
  Neuropsychology. | Neurosciences.
Classification: LCC RC506 .N669 2023 (print) | LCC RC506
  (ebook) | DDC 616.89/17—dc23/eng/20221007
LC record available at https://lccn.loc.gov/2022038693
LC ebook record available at https://lccn.loc.gov/2022038694

ISBN: 978-0-367-67804-3 (hbk)
ISBN: 978-0-367-67807-4 (pbk)
ISBN: 978-1-003-13290-5 (ebk)

DOI: 10.4324/9781003132905

Typeset in Times New Roman
by Apex CoVantage, LLC

Contents

Introduction

> Every attempt to discover a localization of mental processes . . .
> has miscarried completely. The same fate would await any the-
> ory that attempted to recognize the anatomical position of the
> system (consciousness) – as being in the cortex, and to localize
> the unconscious processes in the subcortical parts of the brain.
> There is a hiatus which at present cannot be filled, nor is it one
> of the tasks of psychology to fill it. Our psychical topography
> has for the present nothing to do with anatomy.
>
> (Freud 1915)

Overview and main goal of the book

Mismatch between psyche and brain – different models in psychoanalysis and neuroscience

How can we link psychoanalysis to neuroscience? Freud himself tried
to connect psychoanalysis and neuroscience in his early writing "Project of a Scientific Psychology" (1895). However, in the following,
he gave up on such a project, focusing mainly on the development
of psychoanalysis. These efforts flare up again our time, including
various clusters of recent neuroscientific research. One cluster is the
"embodied brain hypothesis" that conceives cognitive and affective
functions of the brain as closely linked to the body and its interoceptive functions. This has led to concepts like "embodied remembering", "embodied unconscious", "embodied memories", "embodied
feelings", and "embodied testimony" (Leuzinger-Bohleber 2018;
Edelman 1987, 1989, 1992; Mucci 2019; Northoff 2011, 2012a).

DOI: 10.4324/9781003132905-1

Yet another cluster of neuroscientific research is the dynamic neuropsychology by AR Lurija that, through Solms' clinical-anatomical localization approach to psychodynamic features, provides one link of brain and psyche. Moreover, in addition to cognitive neuroscience, the development of affective neuroscience by especially Jaak Panksepp (1998) represents another cluster where primary and secondary emotions are linked to primary and secondary processes (Panksepp and Biven 2012; Solms 2015). Finally, yet another more recent cluster is developed by Mark Solms when he aims to link the free energy and predictive coding approach by Karl Friston to psychoanalysis: he considers the biologically and physically defined concepts of free energy and predictive coding to reflect what Freud referred to as mental or psychical energy (Solms 2020, 2021; Solms and Friston 2018). That, according to Solms, provides the key connection of brain and psyche as core feature of a "new project for a scientific psychology" (Solms 2020, 2021).

Despite all progress, neuroscientific approaches adhere to a scientific psychology that, as traditionally conceived, is based on specific functions and the third-person perspective. Just as the psyche is in psychology, the brain is conceived in terms of specific functions showing extrinsic contents, affective, cognitive, or social: these are localized in particular regions of the brain, remain the same over time, and are investigated by probing the brain's task-related activity. As in the case of the psyche in psychology, this amounts largely to a non-energetic, mostly static, content-based, and third-person–based view of the brain.

Psychoanalysis, in both its original inception and current manifestations, contends such a view of the psyche as presupposed in psychology. Instead, the psyche is conceived as highly energetic (like cathexis) rather than non-energetic; it is continuously changing and thus dynamic rather than static, exhibits a structure or organization that shapes its contents, and aims for a first- or second- rather than third-person–based view of the psyche (e.g., Schilbach 2010; Northoff et al. 2007; Przyrembel et al. 2012; Longo and Tsakiris 2013). This leaves a gap, a "gap of contingency", when compared to the current view of the brain in neuroscience: the energetic, dynamic, structural/organizational, and first-/second-person features of the psyche in psychoanalysis are related to a brain that is non-energetic, static, content based, and third-person based.

Such a mismatch between the models of psyche (in psychoanalysis) and brain (in affective, cognitive, and social neuroscience) renders it impossible to take into view their intimate connection, that is, how neural activity transforms into psychic activity. Our view of brain-psyche is consequently blocked by a gap, with their connection remaining contingent (rather than necessary a posteriori; Northoff 2018) – I will therefore speak later of a "gap of contingency".

"Common currency" of brain and psyche – topography and dynamic

How can we close the "gap of contingency" between brain and psyche? One way is to take the brain into view in terms that are analogous to the model of the psyche in psychoanalysis. Specifically, one may want to conceive of the brain in terms of its energy, dynamic, structure/topography, and first-/second-person perspective. Brain and psyche can then be conceived of in analogous terms with the ultimate hope that these features are shared by brain and psyche as their "common currency" (Northoff et al. 2020a).

What can such "common currency" consist in? I propose that it consists in the most basic feature of both brain and psyche, namely their own inner time and space. Space is manifest in topography, while time is constituted by change, that is, dynamic. I thus propose that topography and dynamic are shared by both brain and psyche, providing their intimate link, the "common currency". What exactly is meant by that will be developed and sketched in this introduction and applied to various psychodynamic features in the subsequent chapters.

The goal of this book is to provide an overview of neuropsychoanalysis by gaining insight into this more intimate spatiotemporal connection of brain and psyche in a truly dynamic, energetic, and structural way. We will see how such a view of the brain can provide a direct link to various psychodynamic features as discussed in current psychoanalysis like self and narcissism (Chapter 1), attachment and trauma (Chapter 2), defense mechanisms (Chapter 3), cathexis (Chapter 4), unconscious and conscious (Chapter 5), dreams (Chapter 6), schizophrenia and depression (Chapter 7), and even psychodynamic or, better, spatiotemporal psychotherapy (Conclusion).

Given that this book is short, its focus is more on developing the brain–psyche link rather than discussing all the various (neuro)psychoanalytic theories and approaches in full detail. I conclude that this more intimate brain–psyche connection holds the promise of completing Freud's own unfinished attempt to link psychology and neuroscience in his "project for a scientific psychology" (1895), including its more recent variant, Mark Solms' "(new) project for a scientific psychology" (Solms 2020, 2021). I therefore speak of a "project for a spatiotemporal neuroscience" (Northoff and Scalabrini 2021) (Conclusion).

Psychoanalysis and neuroscience – contrasting views of psyche and brain

Psyche in psychoanalysis – dynamic, topographic, and spatio-temporal

One of Freud's key observations was that the psyche is dynamic; that is, it changes over time, with the changes following a certain pattern that establishes a particular structure or organization. The emphasis on the dynamics of the psyche is well reflected in his notion of mental or psychic energy, that is, cathexis, that fuels drives, libido, instinct, and the dynamic unconscious where cathexis remains unconstrained. This mental energy is key in structuring and organizing the psyche in a dynamic way. That is reflected in his first topographical model of the unconscious–conscious as well as in his second topographical model of the three-fold relation of *Id*, *Ego*, and *Super-ego*.

Freud aimed to decipher a deeper and more fundamental layer of the psyche beneath its functions and contents when focusing on its dynamic and topography. How, though, can we describe dynamic and topography of the psyche independently of and prior to their functions and contents? Freud himself emphasizes the spatial and temporal features of the psyche – we may require a spatiotemporal complementing the affective and/or cognitive approach to the psyche. This is well reflected in the following quote by Freud himself.

Accordingly, we will picture the mental apparatus as a compound instrument, to the components of which we will give the name of "agencies", or (for the sake of greater clarity) "systems". It is to be anticipated, in the next place, that these systems may perhaps stand in a regular spatial relation to one another, in the same kind of way in which the various systems of lenses in a telescope are arranged behind one another. Strictly speaking, there is no need for the hypothesis that the psychical systems are actually arranged in a *spatial* order. It would be sufficient if a fixed order were established by the fact that in a given psychical process the excitation passes through the systems in a particular *temporal* sequence. In other processes the sequence may perhaps be a different one; that is a possibility that we shall leave open. For the sake of brevity we will in future speak of the components of the apparatus as "ψ-systems"

(Freud 1900, 535; emphasis added)

Psyche in psychology – static, modular, and non-spatiotemporal

The conception of the psyche in psychoanalysis by dynamic, topography, and spatiotemporal features stands in contrast to the view of the static view of the psyche. The psyche is often conceived as a collection of functions in terms of modules that are merely added together, standing side by side in parallel. For instance, different memory systems (like working, semantic, and episodic memory), as well as distinct emotions or form of attention, are distinguished from each other operating more or less independently or in a modular way. Accordingly, there is no assumption of an overall psychic structure, that is, topography encompassing all functions in an organized whole.

Moreover, the various psychological functions are considered stable and non-changing, thus being static – the dynamic beneath the functions is thus often neglected. Together, this amounts to a view of the psyche in psychology in terms of functions and their contents, while their underlying spatial and temporal features are neglected. This stands in contrast to the view of the psyche in psychoanalysis, where spatial and temporal features are assumed to shape and constitute the psyche (see previously).

Finally, there is also a methodological difference between psychoanalysis and psychology regarding first-/second- vs. third-person perspective. Psychoanalysis requires first-/second-person reports with subjective experience for understanding the dynamic manifestations of psychic energy as well as the structure of conscious–unconscious and *Id–Ego–Super-Ego*, that is, their topography. That stands in contrast to psychology. Here, the focus is on objective observation in third-person perspective so as to eclipse and exclude any traces of subjective first/second perspective. Even stronger, first-/second-person experience is often criticized as non-scientific in conventional psychology that focuses strictly on third-person perspective to acquire data. Hence, the dynamic vs static approaches to the psyche stand in opposition and are exclusive on methodological grounds. This makes a more comprehensive and holistic approach more urgent.

View of the brain in cognitive, affective, and social neuroscience – static, regional-modular, and non-spatiotemporal

Neuroscience and its different branches, like cognitive, affective, social, and cultural (just to name a few), are developed largely as extensions of the respective branches in psychology. This means that the static, modular, non-spatial, non-temporal, and third-person–based view of the psyche is more or less transferred to the brain itself.

Particular cognitive or affective functions are associated with specific brain regions whose neural activity, as related to these functions, is conceived of as non-changing, that is, static and modular, that is, localized in specific brain regions (like the localization of primary and secondary emotions in distinct subcortical and cortical regions; Panksepp 1998). The brain itself and its neural activity are consequently conceived of as static, modular, non-spatiotemporal, and third-person based. This view of the brain, although necessary for the discovery of brain-related functions and contents, predominates in current cognitive and affective neuroscience (and related branches like social and cultural neuroscience) and lacks a more holistic and comprehensive approach.

The primacy of functions and contents goes along with a focus on task-related activity that measures the impact of the former on the brain's neural activity. Analogously to the functions themselves, task-related activity is then also considered in a static and regional-modular way independently of potentially underlying spatial and temporal features. Taken together, cognitive and affective neuroscience (and their various siblings) consider the brain and its task-related activity in more or less the same terms as the psyche is viewed in psychology.

Given such an analogy in their characterization, the brain and its task-related activity are supposed to account for the psyche, thus bridging the gap between neuroscience and psychology. In contrast, such a view of the brain does not bridge the gap to the view of the psyche in psychoanalysis, as that is dynamic, topographic, and spatiotemporal rather than static, modular, and non-spatiotemporal.

"Common currency" of brain and psyche – topography and dynamic

"Common currency" – temporal dynamic and spatial topography are shared by brain and psyche

How can cognitive, social, and affective neuroscience account for the psychodynamic view of the psyche? The various clusters of their connection pointed out in this introduction cannot but suffer from a fundamental discrepancy between brain and psyche. They all aim to connect a static, regional-modular, and non-spatiotemporal brain, featuring its extrinsic task-related activity, with a dynamic, topographic, and spatiotemporal psyche characterized by its intrinsic spontaneity. The only way to remedy this discrepancy is to view the brain in a way that is analogous to the psyche in psychoanalysis. The brain and its neural activity may thus need to be conceived as dynamic, topographic, and spatiotemporal – this is the aim of what recently has been introduced as "spatiotemporal neuroscience" (Northoff et al. 2020a, 2020b).

One key feature of the brain is its spontaneous activity that refers to the absence of specific tasks or stimuli as can be measured during the resting state (Logothetis et al. 2009; Northoff 2012b, 2014a, 2014b, 2018; Raichle 2009, 2010). The spontaneous activity can be characterized topographically by various interacting networks like default-mode network, salience network, central executive network, and so on, whose relationships seem to be modulated by the brain's global activity, that is, global signal topography (Scalabrini et al. 2020;

Zhang et al. 2020; Tanabe et al. 2020), while on the temporal side, the brain's spontaneous activity is characterized by fluctuations or oscillations in various frequency ranges (see the following for details) that, together, provide a certain temporal dynamic structure (Buzsaki 2006; Northoff 2018; He 2014; Scalabrini et al. 2017, 2019).

The spontaneous activity itself has recently been associated with various internally oriented cognitive functions like mind wandering (Christoff et al. 2016; Smallwood and Schooler 2015; Northoff 2018), mental time travel or episodic simulation (Schacter et al. 2012; Northoff 2017), autobiographical memory, and self-referential processing (Northoff et al. 2006; Northoff 2016). Hence, the spatial topography of the spontaneous activity may itself be related to different forms of cognition (Smallwood et al. 2021; Yeshurun et al. 2021). This leaves open how the spontaneous activity mediates such cognitive (and also affective and social) functions during both resting state and task-related activity, though. Addressing this question is key in providing an intimate connection of the brain and cognition/emotion, that is, of neural and psychological activity and hence of brain and psyche.

We postulate that, in order to provide such an intimate connection, brain and psyche must share some features, a "common currency" (Northoff et al. 2020a, 2020b). Freud's topography and dynamic of the psyche entail a spatial and temporal view of the psyche: the temporal and spatial organization and structure of the psyche shape its contents and functions. Relying on Freud and our spatiotemporal characterization of the brain's spontaneous activity, we now propose that spatial topography and temporal dynamic are shared by both neural and psychic activity. What Freud described as mental topography and dynamic of the psyche also characterizes, in more or less analogous ways, the brain's neural activity, including both spontaneous and task-related activity. Spatial topography and temporal dynamic are thus shared as "common currency" of brain and psyche (Northoff et al. 2020a, 2020b).

View of the brain in spatiotemporal neuroscience – dynamic, topographic, and spatiotemporal

We are now ready to determine what we recently introduced as "spatiotemporal neuroscience" (Northoff et al. 2020a, 2020b). As explicated previously, cognitive and affective (and social and cultural neuroscience) largely view the brain as static, regional-modular, and non-spatiotemporal. This contrasts with spatiotemporal neuroscience, which conceives the brain's neural activity (including both spontaneous and task-related activity) largely in dynamic, topographic, and spatiotemporal terms.

Rather than the neural activity of affective, cognitive, and so on functions and contents themselves, the focus in spatiotemporal neuroscience is on the spatial topography and temporal dynamic of their neural activity during both internally and externally oriented cognition. Spatiotemporal neuroscience thus conceives both the brain's neural activity and the psyche's mental activity primarily in spatial-topographic and temporal-dynamic terms: it focuses on the brain's spatial and temporal features that constitute its dynamic and topography and how they, in turn, shape cognitive, affective, and social brain function including their respective contents. This makes it clear that spatiotemporal neuroscience neither stands contradictory to nor is exclusive to affective, cognitive, and social neuroscience. Instead, the former integrates and embeds the latter in a broader, more comprehensive spatial and temporal context, that is, topography and dynamic.

The same also applies to predictive coding and free energy. Spatiotemporal neuroscience provides the spatial-topographic and temporal-dynamic context within which predictive coding and free energy operate; they provide what has been called "deep temporal model" (Kiebel et al. 2008; Friston et al. 2017) or "temporal thickness" (Seth 2015). The same applies to the link of first and third person. Spatiotemporal neuroscience takes into consideration first-person experience of mental features and links them to third-person observation about the brain – this link is made possible through spatiotemporal features being shared by both first and third person as their "common currency". This shall now be demonstrated by various examples of different psychodynamic features, as laid out in the subsequent chapters.

References

Buzsaki G (2006) Rhythms of the brain. Oxford University Press, Oxford. doi: 10.1093/acprof:oso/9780195301069.001.0001

Christoff K, Irving ZC, Fox KC, Spreng RN, Andrews-Hanna JR (2016) Mind-wandering as spontaneous thought: A dynamic framework. Nat Rev Neurosci. 17(11):718–731. doi: 10.1038/nrn.2016.113

Edelman GM (1987) Neural Darwinism: The theory of neuronal group selection. Basic Books, New York.

Edelman GM (1989) The remembered present: A biological theory of consciousness. Basic Books, New York.

Edelman GM (1992) Bright air, brilliant fire: On the matter of the mind. Basic Books, New York.

Freud S (1895) Project for a scientific psychology. Hogarth Press, London.

Freud S (1900) The interpretation of dreams (SE, Vols. 4 & 5). Hogarth Press, London.

Freud S (1915) The unconscious (SE, Vol. 14, pp. 166–204). Hogarth Press, London.

Friston KJ, Parr T, de Vries B (2017) The graphical brain: Belief propagation and active inference. Netw Neurosci. 1(4):381–414. doi: 10.1162/NETN_a_00018

He BJ (2014) Scale-free brain activity: Past, present, and future. Trends Cogn Sci. 18(9):480–487. doi: 10.1016/j.tics.2014.04.003

Kiebel SJ, Daunizeau J, Friston KJ (2008) A hierarchy of time-scales and the brain. PLoS Comput Biol. 4(11):e1000209. doi: 10.1371/journal.pcbi.1000209

Leuzinger-Bohleber M (2018) Finding the body in the mind: Embodied memories, trauma, and depression. Routledge, Abingdon, UK.

Logothetis NK, Murayama Y, Augath M, Steffen T, Werner J, Oeltermann A (2009) How not to study spontaneous activity. Neuroimage. 45(4):1080–1089. doi: j.neuroimage.2009.01.010

Longo MR, Tsakiris M (2013) Merging second-person and first-person neuroscience. The Behavioral and Brain Sciences. 36(4):429. doi: 10.1017/S0140525X12001975

Mucci C (2019) Traumatization through human agency: "Embodied witnessing" is essential in the treatment of survivors. Am. J. Psychoanal. 79:540–554. doi: 10.1057/s11231-019-09225-y

Northoff G (2011) Neuropsychoanalysis in practice: Brain, self and objects. Oxford University Press, Oxford.

Northoff G (2012a) Psychoanalysis and the brain: Why did Freud abandon neuroscience? Front. Psychol. 3:71. doi: 10.3389/fpsyg.2012.00071

Northoff G (2012b) Immanuel Kant's mind and the brain's resting state. Trends Cogn Sci. 16(7):356–359. doi: 10.1016/j.tics.2012.06.001

Northoff G (2014a) Unlocking the brain: Volume 1 coding. Oxford University Press, Oxford. doi: 10.1093/acprof:oso/9780199826988.001.0001

Northoff G (2014b) Unlocking the brain: Volume 2 consciousness. Oxford University Press, Oxford. doi: 10.1093/acprof:oso/9780199826995.001.0001

Northoff G (2016) Is the self a higher-order or fundamental function of the brain? The "basis model of self-specificity" and its encoding by the brain's spontaneous activity. Cogn. Neurosci. 7(1–4):203–222. doi: 10.1080/17588928.2015.1111868

Northoff G (2017) Personal identity and cortical midline structure (CMS): Do temporal features of CMS neural activity transform into "self-continuity"? Psychol. Inq. 28(2–3):122–131. doi: 10.1080/1047840X.2017.1337396

Northoff G (2018) The spontaneous brain: From the mind-body to the world-brain problem. MIT Press, Cambridge, MA. doi: 10.7551/mitpress/9780262038072.001.0001

Northoff G, Bermpohl F, Schoeneich F, Boeker H (2007) How does our brain constitute defense mechanisms? First-person neuroscience and psychoanalysis. Psychother Psychosom. 76(3):141–153. doi: 10.1159/000099841

Northoff G, Heinzel A, De Greck M, Bermpohl F, Dobrowolny H, Panksepp J (2006) Self-referential processing in our brain: A meta-analysis of imaging studies on the self. Neuroimage. 31(1):440–457. doi: 10.1016/j.neuroimage.2005.12.002

Northoff G, Scalabrini A (2021) "Project for a spatiotemporal neuroscience" – Brain and psyche share their topography and dynamic. Front Psychol. Oct 14;12:717402. doi: 10.3389/fpsyg.2021.717402. eCollection 2021.

Northoff G, Wainio-Theberge S, Evers K (2020a) Is temporo-spatial dynamics the "common currency" of brain and mind? In quest of "spatiotemporal neuroscience". Phys. Life Rev. 33:34–54. doi: 10.1016/j.plrev.2019.05.002

Northoff G, Wainio-Theberge S, Evers K (2020b) Spatiotemporal neuroscience: What is it and why we need it. Phys. Life Rev. 33:78–87. doi: 10.1016/j.plrev.2020.06.005

Panksepp J (1998) The periconscious substrates of consciousness: Affective states and the evolutionary origins of the self. J. Conscious. Stud. 5:566–582.

Panksepp J, Biven L (2012) The archaeology of mind: Neuroevolutionary origins of human emotions (Norton Series on Interpersonal Neurobiology). WW Norton & Company, New York.

Przyrembel M, Smallwood J, Pauen M, Singer T (2012) Illuminating the dark matter of social neuroscience: Considering the problem of social interaction from philosophical, psychological, and neuroscientific perspectives. Front. Hum. Neurosci. 6:190. doi.org/10.3389/fnhum.2012.00190

Raichle ME (2009) A paradigm shift in functional brain imaging. J. Neurosci. 29(41):12729–12734. doi: 10.1523/JNEUROSCI.4366-09.2009

Raichle ME (2010) Two views of brain function. Trends Cogn Sci. 14(4):180–190. doi: 10.1016/j.tics.2010.01.008

Scalabrini A, Ebisch SJH, Huang Z, Di Plinio S, Perrucci MG, Romani GL, et al (2019) Spontaneous brain activity predicts task-evoked activity during animate versus inanimate touch. Cereb. Cortex. 29:4628–4645. doi: 10.1093/cercor/bhy340

Scalabrini A, Huang Z, Mucci C, Perrucci MG, Ferretti A, Fossati A, et al (2017) How spontaneous brain activity and narcissistic features shape social interaction. Sci. Rep. 7:9986. doi: 10.1038/s41598-017-10389-9

Scalabrini A, Vai B, Poletti S, Damiani S, Mucci C, Colombo C, Zanardi R, Benedetti F, Northoff G (2020) All roads lead to the default-mode network: Global source of DMN abnormalities in major depressive disorder. Neuropsychopharmacology. 45(12):2058–2069. doi: 10.1038/s41386-020-0785-x

Schacter DL, Addis DR, Hassabis D, Martin VC, Spreng RN, Szpunar KK (2012) The future of memory: Remembering, imagining, and the brain. Neuron. 76(4):677–694. doi: 10.1016/j.neuron.2012.11.001

Schilbach L (2010) A second-person approach to other minds. Nat Rev Neurosci. 11:449. doi: 10.1038/nrn2805-c1

Seth AK (2015) Neural coding: Rate and time codes work together. Curr Biol. 25(3):R110–R113. doi: 10.1016/j.cub.2014.12.043

Smallwood J, Bernhardt BC, Leech R, Bzdok D, Jefferies E, Margulies DS (2021) The default mode network in cognition: A topographical perspective. Nat. Rev. Neurosci. 1–11. doi: 10.1038/s41583-021-00474-4

Smallwood J, Schooler JW (2015) The science of mind wandering: Empirically navigating the stream of consciousness. Annu Rev Psychol. 66:487–518. doi: 10.1146/annurev-psych-010814-015331

Solms M (2015) Reconsolidation: Turning consciousness into memory. Behav. Brain Sci. 38. doi: 10.1017/S0140525X14000296

Solms M (2020) New project for a scientific psychology: General scheme. Neuropsychoanalysis. 22:5–35. doi: 10.1080/15294145.2020.1833361

Solms M (2021) The hidden spring: A journey to the source of consciousness. WW Norton & Company, New York.

Solms M, Friston K (2018) How and why consciousness arises: Some considerations from physics and physiology. J. Conscious. Stud. 25:202–238.

Tanabe S, Huang Z, Zhang J, Chen Y, Fogel S, Doyon J, Wu J, Xu J, Zhang J, Qin P, Wu X, Mao Y, Mashour GA, Hudetz AG, Northoff G (2020) Altered global brain signal during physiologic, pharmacologic, and pathologic states of unconsciousness in humans and rats. Anesthesiology. 132(6):1392–1406. doi: 10.1097/ALN.0000000000003197

Yeshurun Y, Nguyen M, Hasson U (2021) The default mode network: Where the idiosyncratic self meets the shared social world. Nat Rev Neurosci. 22(3):181–192. doi: 10.1038/s41583-020-00420-w

Zhang J, Huang Z, Tumati S, Northoff G (2020) Rest-task modulation of fMRI-derived global signal topography is mediated by transient coactivation patterns. PLoS Biol. 18(7):e3000733. doi: 10.1371/journal.pbio.3000733

Chapter 1

Self and narcissism

Introduction

One of the key discoveries of Freud and subsequent psychoanalysis
is that the ego is not a homogenous entity. Instead, the ego refers
to a particular structure or organization, the famous three-fold
structure or topography of Id, Ego, and Super-ego. There has been
much discussion about this and further developments in subsequent
psychoanalysis up to the present day. Instead of recounting these
developments in psychoanalysis, we rather focus on whether there
are corresponding developments in neuroscience that may able to
integrate both psychological and neural observations.

The core of the ego is the self, which is considered intrinsically
subjective. The self has been extensively investigated for its neural
correlates in neuroscience in recent years. This includes different
concepts of self like mental self, bodily self, objective vs subjective self, integrative self, emotional self, and so on (Northoff 2016;
Frewen et al. 2020; Qin et al. 2020; Sui and Humphreys 2015 for
overviews). The different concepts of self are often associated with
distinct regions or networks in the brain. Core regions include especially the regions in the middle of the brain, the cortical (and also
subcortical) midline structures (CMS), which are the center of the
default-mode network (DMN).

How are psychodynamic and neuroscientific concepts of self
related to each other? David Milrod points out an essential difference between neuroscientific and psychoanalytic concepts of self.
Neuroscience and psychology focus more on the universal and

DOI: 10.4324/9781003132905-2

objective features of self, namely that which is shared among all subjects. Psychoanalysis, in contrast, tends to take into view more the intra-psychic, inter-subjective, and subjective features of self:

> In short, they (neuroscience and psychology) concern themselves with the universal and objective. Psychoanalysis, which has historically focused on the individual (rather than the universal) and has been interested more in ontology (rather than the empirical), has as its goal the understanding of protracted intrapsychic, interpersonal, and subjective functioning of the individual.
>
> (Milrod 2002, 22–23)

The present chapter aims to connect subjective (as in psychoanalysis as the subjective core of the ego) and objective (as in neuroscience with objective neural correlates) features of self. For that, topography and dynamics are assumed to provide the bridge – spatial topography and temporal dynamics provide the shared feature or "common currency" of objective brain and subjective self. The first part will focus on the spatial topography of self as complemented by the temporal dynamics of self in the second part. The third part will focus on narcissism and its recent findings in neuroscience.

Part I: spatial topography – nestedness as "common currency" of brain and self

Topography mediates the transition from brain to psyche – spatial layers and nested hierarchy

Topography refers to a particular spatial organization or structure of brain and psyche. One key feature of their topographies are hierarchies. Hierarchies have been postulated in both neuroscience and psychoanalysis. They may thus offer insight into the intimate connection of, for instance, brain and self. The English neurologist Hughling Jackson early on proposed a three-layer hierarchy of the brain's regions with lower, middle, and higher centers that were assumed to be associated with different psychological functions (see Wiest 2012 for an overview). More recently, Panksepp (1998, 2012) conceived the brain's subcortical–cortical organization and associated its different layers with different levels of emotions (like primary, secondary, and tertiary emotions) (see also Northoff et al. 2011). Extending the limbic system to the cortical level, Northoff (Northoff et al. 2011) pursued a more radial-concentric approach with three layers of self, that is, bodily, affective, and cognitive. We will see that, together with the recent data, this supports the idea of a spatially nested hierarchy of self based on the brain's radial-concentric cortical organization.

A clearly hierarchical organization of self (the term is used here in a broader sense) that embeds and contains the concept of ego has also been proposed in psychology/psychoanalysis by Freud. For instance, Kernberg (1984) noted how Freud preserved the Ego not only as a mental structure and psychic agency but also as the subjective experiential self in all his writings. Freud suggested the Id to be the lowest level of the topography of the psyche that remains essentially unconscious but nevertheless strongly influences the upper levels of the Ego and the Super-ego.

Together, this amounts to a nested hierarchy of self where the lower layer somewhat resurfaces within the next upper layer and so forth (see also Wiest 2012). While Freud's rigid three-layer partition was criticized later by others, the multi-facedness of self with its sense of subjectivity permeating across its bodily, affective, and cognitive layers remains a key feature in both neuroscience and psychoanalysis. We will demonstrate that the model of a nested hierarchy of self is strongly supported by recent neuroscience in both its spatial and temporal aspects – therefore, we characterize the neural and psychological hierarchy of self by spatial and temporal nestedness.

Topography of self I – interoceptive layer and the inner bodily self

A recent large-scale meta-analysis in healthy subjects by Qin et al. (2020) investigated and analyzed different imaging studies that focused on different aspects of self, inner body (interoceptive), outer body (extero-proprioceptive), and own cognitive or mental states. They observed different regions to be associated with each of the three layers; at the same time, there was regional overlap, as the regions of the lower layer were included within the next upper layer (see subsequently for details). Together, this amounts to a spatial multi-layered nested hierarchical model of self (Qin et al. 2020), including (i) interoceptive self, (ii) extero-proprioceptive self, and (iii) mental self. This shall be detailed in the following.

The interoceptive self refers to how the brain process the body's inner organs and their inputs, resulting in our perception of our own inner body. This can be investigated through fMRI task studies that measure interoceptive awareness of one's own body, including cardio-respiratory awareness and urogenital and gastro-intestinal awareness. That was complemented by extero-proprioceptive self fMRI studies focusing on external bodily inputs like facial or proprioceptive inputs connected to the self. Finally, fMRI studies also included the "typical" more cognitive mental self fMRI studies employing trait adjectives or other stimuli where subjects have to become aware of their own self (like their own name or picture) as distinct from others.

Based on the interoceptive studies, there is a most basic or lower layer of self, an interoceptive self that is related to regions that mostly process interoceptive stimuli from the own body, that is, bilateral insula, dorsal anterior cingulate cortex, thalamus, and parahippocampus, thus including mainly regions of the salience network (Menon 2011; Qin et al. 2020). The fact that these regions were shared among the different kinds of interoceptive awareness, that is, cardiorespiratory, urogenital, and gastrointestinal, suggests that these regions are key in integrating different interoceptive inputs of the various organs of the inner body (Craig 2003, 2010). One can thus speak of an "interoceptive or vegetative self" (Babo-Rebelo et al. 2016, 2019; Tsakiris 2017), "bodily self" (Damasio 2010), or "proto-self" (Panksepp 1998) as the most basic and fundamental layer of self.

Topography of self II – exteroceptive and mental layers

The next or middle layer of self includes what Qin et al. (2020) describe as proprioceptive or exteroceptive self; the fMRI studies focusing on external bodily related inputs like facial or proprioceptive inputs yielded regions like interior frontal gyrus, premotor cortex, temporo-parietal junction (TPJ), and medial prefrontal cortex (MPFC), as well as the regions of the interoceptive layer, that is, insula, thalamus, and anterior cingulate. As these regions process inputs from different sensory modalities, they may be key in not only integrating extero- and proprioceptive modalities but also different exteroceptive sensory modalities, that is, cross-modal integration. Despite their differences, these regions share the processing of proprioceptive inputs related to the own body – one can thus speak of a "proprio- or exteroceptive self, or embodied self" (Tsakiris 2017; Gallagher 2005; Panksepp 1998; Damasio 2010).

Finally, the most upper layer of self (Qin et al. 2020) is based on fMRI studies that yielded typical DMN midline regions like medial prefrontal cortex and posterior cingulate cortex as well as the regions included in the second level, most notably bilateral TPJ, and first level, bilateral insula and thalamus. These regions seem to be recruited when one needs to represent one's own self in mental states – one can therefore also speak of a "mental or cognitive self" (Qin et al. 2020) or "extended self" (Damasio 2010).

Together, these findings suggest what Qin et al. (2020) describe as "nested hierarchy of self": regions of the lower level were included in the next higher level where they were complemented by additional regions and so forth. For instance, bilateral insula was present on the most basic level, that is, the interoceptive self, and resurfaced (in completely independent imaging studies) again in both the second, that is, proprioceptive self, and third, that is, mental self, levels. The same holds true for the bilateral TPJ, which first showed in the intermediate layer of the proprioceptive self and re-resurfaced again in the third level of the mental self. Accordingly, each of the hierarchical levels of self recruits both overlapping and separate regions compared to the other levels, amounting to a spatially nested hierarchy of self.

Topography of brain and ego – spatial nestedness as their "common currency"

Freud and psychoanalysis target a deeper layer of the mind. Rather than focusing on the conscious at the surface, they venture into the unconscious depth of our psyche. This led him and others to assume that our mind constitutes a certain hierarchy or structure of the ego. We can now see that the ego's subjective core, that is, its self, exhibits a certain structure, which may be based on the brain's structure, that is, its topography with the distinct layers of self. This converges with the unconscious nature of the deeper subjective layers of the ego and the mind in general that Freud and psychoanalysis describe so well.

Similar to the unconscious mind, we have no access to the deeper layers of our brain itself; that is, we remain unable to become conscious of our brain's topography as such. Its topographical organization remains unconscious if not non-conscious for us. All we can become conscious of is the self in its distinct manifestations, interoceptive, exteroceptive, and cognitive-mental, while its underlying organization, its topography, is precluded from our consciousness, thus remaining unconscious if not non-conscious.

One may now want to raise the question of whether the two topographies of Freud, his first about the ego and his second about the conscious, converge with the topography of the brain and its self sketched here. Obviously, it is tempting to associate the three layers of ego, Id, Ego, and Super-ego, with the three layers of the brain's topography, interoceptive, exteroceptive, and cognitive-mental, respectively.

However, that is complicated by the fact that the tripartite structure of the ego is far from well established even within psychoanalysis itself. Moreover, on the neuroscience side, future studies may want to refine the brain-based three-layered nested organization of the self by including sub-layers and a more sophisticated differentiation of the distinct layers of self. In particular, the notion of nestedness needs to be refined in both conceptual and empirical terms.

Though preliminarily at this point, we can nevertheless say that there are converging developments in psychoanalysis and neuroscience. Both approach the ego (or self) in terms of structure and organization and thus more generally signify them by topography. The brain-based topography of self in neuroscience holds the promise to converge with the topography of the ego in psychoanalysis. If future studies can reveal similar or analogous topography of both psychodynamic models of ego and neuroscientific models of self, the respective topographical organization may be shared by both brain and psyche as their "common currency" (Northoff et al. 2020a, 2020b). Albeit tentatively, awaiting further specification, we here assume that spatial nestedness, the resurfacing of lower layers within the upper layers, may be conceived of as a strong candidate to serve as the "common currency" of the topographies of brain and ego.

Part II: temporal dynamic – scalefreeness as "common currency" of brain and self

Dynamic of the brain – operation across different timescales in a scale-free way

We have seen the spatial organization of the brain and how that relates to its self. In addition to the spatial side, there is also the temporal dimension, the dynamic of self, that is, how it changes inherently over time. We will see that, analogously to the spatial side, there is also a particular temporal structure or organization in the dynamic of the brain. That temporal structure, in turn, is closely related to the self.

The brain's spontaneous neural activity can be characterized by different fluctuations or waves, with frequencies ranging from infraslow (0.01–0.1 Hz), over slow (0.1–1 hz), fast (1–40 Hz), and ultrafast (40–180 Hz; Buzsaki 2006). Power is strongest in the infraslow range and decreases across the slow, fast, and ultrafast ranges following a power law distribution (He 2014; He et al. 2010; Huang et al. 2016). Together, the different frequencies and their distinct degrees of power constitute a complex temporal structure in the brain's spontaneous activity, which, in large parts, can feature the balance between infraslow, slow, and faster frequencies.

The relationship between these frequencies is maintained across different temporal scales and can therefore be characterized by what is described as "scale-free dynamics" (He et al. 2010; He 2014; Linkenkaer-Hansen et al. 2001). Roughly, scale-free activity describes the fractal (i.e., self-similar) organization and thus temporal nestedness in the relationship between power and the different frequency ranges: the longer and more powerful slower frequencies nest and contain the shorter and less powerful faster frequencies – this amounts to long-range temporal correlation (LRTC), which operates across different time scales or frequencies (Northoff and Huang 2017; Linkenkaer-Hansen et al. 2001; He 2014; He et al. 2010).

LRTC makes it possible to assess the degree to which past neuronal patterns exert their influence on future dynamics, thus accounting for LRTC (Linkenkaer-Hansen et al. 2001; Northoff and Huang 2017). That amounts to a form of memory that is not defined by specific contents that are encoded, stored, and recalled or retrieved. Instead, memory refers here to the structure, the temporal structure, of the neural activity across distinct time points. Being temporal and dynamic, LRTC and its scale-free activity provide not only temporal stability through their correlation of different timescales, that is, temporal continuity, but also temporal memory, that is, temporal stability, through connecting past, future, and present timepoints. One could thus speak of temporal or dynamic memory that, as process- and structure-based memory, must be distinguished from the more content-based cognitive memory in the traditional sense (Northoff 2017; Hasson et al. 2015).

The dynamic of self – the brain's long-range temporal correlations shape the self

Is the self related to the LRTC of the brain's neural activity? Recent studies have shown that the brain's scale-free activity, as measured with the power law exponent (PLE), is related to mental features such as the self (Huang et al. 2016; Scalabrini et al. 2017, 2019; Wolff et al. 2019). Together, these studies show that the degree of resting state PLE directly predicts: (i) the degree of self-consciousness (Huang et al. 2016; Wolff et al. 2019), (ii) task-related activity during self-specific stimuli (Scalabrini et al. 2019), and (iii) the degree of temporal integration on a psychological level of self-specificity (Kolvoort et al. 2020).

Let us describe the findings in more detail. Huang et al. (2016) and Wolff et al. (2018) recorded resting-state activity in fMRI and EEG of the brain, that is, a task-free condition without any external demands. They calculated the degree of the brain's PLE in both fMRI and EEG. The same subjects also underwent psychological investigation of their self with the self-consciousness scale. Both studies found the same relationship of brain PLE and self-consciousness:

the higher the PLE, that is, the more the slow–fast power balance is shifted towards the slower pole, the higher the degree of the subject's private self-consciousness. Importantly, these findings hold only for the PLE as index of slow–fast balance but not for the power of either the slow or fast frequencies alone. Hence it is really the temporal structure and thus the hierarchy of slow–fast power that is related to the self (rather than the single frequencies: power itself).

Finally, it shall be mentioned that this concerns a wide range of frequencies, from very slow (0.01 to 0.1 Hz), as covered by fMRI (Huang et al. 2016), to faster ones as measured in EEG (1–80 Hz) (Wolff et al. 2018). This means that the degree of slow–fast integration, that is, their degree of scale-freeness, is related to the sense of self. The self is thus intrinsically scale free, as it connects and links different timescales, short/fast and long/slow. Such cross-scale self exhibits both temporal continuity and discontinuity by nesting different timescales within each other in a scale-free way: temporal continuity, as mediated by the more powerful slower frequencies, nests and contains temporal discontinuity, as related to the less powerful faster frequencies.

Is such self-specificity of the brain's internal resting state activity also carried over to external task demands during self-specific tasks? This was studied in fMRI by Scalabrini et al. (2017, 2019). They measured both rest as well as task during the active touch towards animate (another person) and non-animate (mannequin hand) targets. They observed that the degree of PLE in the resting state predicted the degree to which subjects could differentiate in their task-related activity between animate and non-animate targets.

Memory and self I – temporal vs cognitive memory

Given that rest and task states occur and are measured at distinct points in time, this strongly suggests a memory effect: the temporal or dynamic memory of the resting state is carried over to the task state, as otherwise the latter could not be modulated by the former. Note that memory is more meant in a temporal way; that is, the temporal continuity (as encoded in the resting state's LRTC) is carried over to the task state and thus to the latter's actual novel external input: the novel input (as during the task state) becomes integrated and entangled within the memory of the ongoing activity (as during the resting state) and its LRTC, that is, its temporal memory.

Psychologically, this means that the novel external stimuli, which remains unrelated to the self, is now integrated with the temporal memory of the latter's LRTC, including its temporal continuity. The degree to which the external input is integrated within the self-based LRTC will determine the degree to which the external input or stimulus, that is, the respective external event, will become self-specific and thus be perceived as being closely related to the self.

Note that the term memory is not understood in a cognitive sense here, that is, in terms of a particular mental content like a particular event (such as a tree falling). Instead, it is understood in a temporal way, the degree to which the resting state with its self-based LRTC is connected with and integrates the external event: this will decide the degree to which we, based on our self, can remember that event, including how much it is connected to our self and affects us. One can thus speak of "process memory" (Hasson et al. 2015) or "temporal memory" (Northoff 2017) which, as reflecting temporal structure, is more structure based than the traditional cognitive view of memory as content based.

Is there more direct empirical support for the resting state's temporal memory of our self and how it shapes external contents? This was addressed by Kolvoort et al. (2020) in an EEG study on self. They measured resting state in EEG and conducted a psychological self-task where subjects were required to associate self- and non-self-specific stimuli across different time delays (from 200 to 1400 ms). They demonstrated that the self-specific effects in terms of accuracy were preserved across all temporal delays with inter-subject variation. That, in turn, was related to the resting state PLE: the higher the resting state PLE, that is, the stronger the slower frequencies relative to the faster ones, the more strongly the self-specific effect was preserved across the different time delays on the psychological level. Together, these findings strongly suggest that the resting state's temporal memory (its LRTC) shapes the temporal integration (and ultimately cognition) of external inputs and events.

Memory and self II – scale-freeness as "common currency"

These findings suggest that temporal integration of different times-cales as indexed by temporal memory may be key in mediating the co-occurrence of temporal stability and flexibility that features our self. The self can thus be characterized by temporal memory that, operating on a deeper layer beneath the traditional content-based cognitive memory, strongly structures and organizes the latter. Albeit tentatively, we assume that such a deeper layer of a structure-based temporal and pre-cognitive form of memory converges well with the more dynamic view of the psyche espoused in psychoanalysis.

While the concept of memory in psychoanalysis is often under-stood in cognitive terms featuring specific contents, that is, uncon-scious and conscious contents, I would like to propose a more dynamic and truly temporal concept of memory: memory is here determined by its temporal structure, its LRTC, that provides tem-poral continuity across different timescales, including short and long. Such temporal memory remains by itself largely unconscious, as we never experience such temporal continuity by itself, that is, independent of any contents in our cognition or mind. The LRTC thus operates at a deeper layer of the brain, just as psychoanalysis assumed that certain events remain unconscious or non-conscious in the depth of our mind.

However, the degree to which that temporal structure, the LRTC of self, is developed strongly shapes the kinds of contents we can recall and remember in our consciousness. For instance, stronger power in slower frequencies (with high LRTC) biases us towards sad contents in our memory, as it is typical of depression, while stronger power in the faster frequencies favors happy and joyful contents, resulting in mania in the most extreme cases. Hence, the deep layer of temporal memory shapes the contents of our cognitive memory.

In sum, we tentatively propose to complement the psychodynamic concept of memory, which strongly relies on the different forms of content-based memory of cognitive neuroscience, by a deeper layer of temporal that, through the brain's LRTC, is structure rather than content based. Such a temporal redefinition of memory is key in providing direct link of the neuronal findings to the psychodynamic observations. Specifically, we tentatively assume that the brain's LRTC on the neuronal level is shared as "common currency" with a more or less corresponding temporal structure of scale-freeness on the cognitive and thus psychological level.

Part III: the self and its narcissism

From self to self-objects – narcissism

One key feature of the self is narcissism. While Freud conceived narcissism in a pathological way as remaining stuck in an earlier sexual and libido-driven developmental stage, Kohut (1977, 1984) considered it an intrinsic feature of our self in general. For that he introduced the notion of self-objects. Kohut points out that self-objects are those objects that are central for constituting and maintaining the self, "a self can never exist outside a matrix of self-objects" (1984, 61). Self-objects provide the self with attachment to and emotion of others: "The self-object concept illuminates a central dimension of human experience: the basic needs for emotional sustenance from others as they emerge and develop through the life cycle" (Gehrie 2009, 48).

Following the previously described brain-based nested hierarchy of self, we may want to consider a nested hierarchy of self-objects. There are the interoceptive self-objects of the own inner body; they are complemented by the proprio-exteroceptive self-objects of the outer body; finally, these two layers are complemented by more abstract cognitive self-objects that are purely mental. The nested hierarchy of self is thus well compatible with the notion of self-objects suggested by Kohut.

The self-objects constitute the matrix for the self and thereby its emotional stability. Hence, if the self-objects themselves become unstable, the self itself becomes unstable, as manifested in emotional instability. How does the self compensate such instability in its own self-objects? One way is to take the self itself as self-object – this results in narcissism. On the neuronal side, such an instability of self-objects may be related to an instability in the nested hierarchy of self with imbalances among the interoceptive, exteroceptive, and cognitive/mental layers of self. This can indeed be supported by recent brain imaging findings.

Topography of narcissism I – empirical findings in insula and other regions

How is the narcissism of self related to the brain's spatial topography and temporal dynamics? Two recent fMRI studies shed some light on this. Fan et al. (2010) combined psychological and neuronal fMRI investigation of a group of healthy subjects with respect to their empathy. They investigated all subjects with a narcissism scale according to which they divided high vs low narcissism subjects. High-narcissism subjects showed higher alexithymia scores, a measure of emotional awareness, and higher general psychiatric symptoms (as on the symptom checklist). This was expected, as it is well known clinically.

The interesting findings were observed in fMRI. Neuronally, the high narcissistic subjects yielded significantly lower degrees of activity changes during the empathy task (compared to non-empathy), especially in the right anterior insula when compared to low narcissism subjects. This is of interest, as the right anterior insula is the region that nests and connects the three distinct layers of self (as described previously). Hence, decreased activity in the right anterior insula may index decreased degrees of connection and nestedness among the three layers of self in highly narcissistic subjects.

Reduced activity change and responsiveness of the right anterior insula as a key region in narcissism could also be observed in another study on healthy subjects and their degree of narcissism (Scalabrini et al. 2017). Here the subjects underwent rest and task fMRIs with the task concerning hand touch of an animate (person) and inanimate (robot) target hand. During the anticipation period of the hand touch, the right anterior insula was activated, which was related to the degree of narcissism: the higher the subjects' degree of narcissism, the lower the degree to which activity in the insula differentiated between the two conditions, that is, animate vs inanimate hand.

Moreover, Scalabrini et al. (2017) showed that the task-related activity in the right insula correlated with the degree of the PLE in the resting: the higher the PLE in rest, that is, the stronger the power in the slower frequencies, the less task-related activity in the insula, with their rest-task relation being mediated by the degree of narcissism (as obtained in the narcissism scale). Together, these findings strongly support the relationship of especially the right anterior insula's temporal dynamics to narcissism, with this region showing less task-related differentiation in its activity during tasks that are relevant to the self like empathy and touching a real or non-real person's hand. Importantly, this seems to be related to the altered temporal dynamic of the right insula, which may thus be a key component contributing to narcissism.

In addition to the insula, other closely related regions like the ventral and dorsal anterior cingulate cortex and the amygdala have been found to be abnormally activated in subjects with high degrees of narcissism (Feng et al. 2018; Jauk et al. 2017; Lou et al. 2021; Chester and DeWall 2016; Nenadic et al. 2015; Mao et al. 2016). These regions are all strongly connected to the insula and implicated in emotion processing, self-referential processing, and also social relation/exclusion, reflecting exactly those dimensions that are typically altered in narcissism.

Topography of narcissism II – imbalance of the brain-based spatial nestedness of self

The findings show that the insula and related emotion regions like the amygdala are abnormally altered in narcissism. We recall that the insula is a key region in the first layer of the self, the interoceptive self, and that it resurfaces in in the subsequent layers of self, the exteroceptive and mental self. In other words, the insula provides the "glue" between the different layers of the nested hierarchy of self. Lower task-related differentiation of the insula means that self and environmental contexts can no longer be properly distinguished anymore in one's experience and perception: the environmental context as the non-self is processed and perceived in terms of the self, resulting in narcissism.

Moreover, the hierarchy of self, with its interoceptive, exteroceptive and mental layers, will become fragile and unstable. This is so because of the nestedness; the interoceptive deficit of the insula will resonate or reverberate throughout the whole nested hierarchy of self to extero-proprioceptive and mental layers of the self. That, in turn, may result in a fragile nested hierarchy of self whose different layers are no longer properly integrated, that is, nested, anymore. The self may thus become unstable, to which it may react with either grandiose self-fantasies with respect to the external world, that is, the thick-skinned type of narcissism, or, alternatively, in a more silent withdrawn and internal way, that is, the more thin-skinned narcissism.

In sum, the spatial nestedness of self may be abnormally shifted in narcissism: the different self-objects can no longer be connected and integrated with each other, which, in turn, threatens the coherent sense of self. Instead of a coherent sense of self with its different layers of self-objects being nested within each other, the different self-objects may no longer properly connect with each other, operating more in parallel rather than in an integrated and nested way. That, in turn, may induce anxiety, as mediated by the close connection of the insula to emotion-mediating regions like amygdala. Moreover, it may abnormally activate especially the mental- or cognitive-layer self (as relayed by the default-mode network with is cortical midline structures) that may then yield the typical narcissistic grandiose fantasies.

Dynamic of narcissism – imbalance of slow and fast frequencies

How about the temporal dynamic in narcissism? There are predominantly fMRI studies on the topography in narcissism but not many studies on its temporal dynamic. One exception is Scalabrini et al. (2017). Investigating healthy subjects, he shows that the insula's resting state's PLE and its modulation of task-related activity are mediated by the degree of narcissism: the stronger the power in the slow frequencies with higher PLE in the resting state of the insula, the less the task-related activity in the insula differs from the ongoing resting state activity.

What does this mean psychologically? Additionally, Scalabrini et al. (2017) observed a correlation of both resting state PLE and task-related activity with the degree of narcissism. The higher the narcissism, the higher the PLE and the lower the task-related activity. Hence, there seems to be clear relationship of rest PLE and task activity with the degree of narcissism. The task consisted in the anticipation of a target, another person's hand. Lower rest-task differentiation with lower task-related activity thus means that the more narcissistic subjects were not able to properly anticipate the next stimulus. Instead, they remained in their own resting state, that is, their own self, remaining unable to reach out to the other.

Importantly, the inability to anticipate reaching out to the other is mediated by the resting state's slow frequencies. The stronger the resting state's slow frequencies in the insula, that is, higher PLE, the less subjects could reach out to the other person. Hence, their intrinsic temporal dynamic is too slow to connect their own self to the other, which requires a faster dynamic. Hence, figuratively speaking, the narcissistic person is too slow to connect their own self with the faster environment, including other selves.

Together, albeit tentatively, the findings suggest altered dynamic in the brain related to the self in narcissism. The dynamic exhibits insufficient fast frequencies in the insula, yielding a rather limited scale-freeness. Changes in scale-freeness constrain the integration of self, including across both its multiple nested layers of self-objects and the scale-free slow–fast dynamics. Together with the spatial findings, this amounts ultimately to decreases in both spatial continuity (across its distinct layers of self-objects) and temporal continuity (across different timescales) of the self in narcissism. We therefore propose a primarily spatiotemporal (rather than cognitive or affective) view of narcissism that determines it by the degree of spatial and temporal nestedness on both neural and psychological levels.

Conclusion

The ego is characterized in psychoanalysis by a particular organization, its three-layered topography. Recent findings in neuroscience show that neuronally, the self, as subjective core of the ego, may also be mediated by a three-layered neural hierarchy of interoceptive, exteroceptive, and mental layers of self. Importantly, these different layers are nested within each other, that is, spatial nestedness. Analogously on the temporal side, one can observe temporal nestedness among slow and fast frequencies whose relationship index the degree of self-consciousness. The balances of both the three spatial layers and the slow–fast dynamic are shifted in their nestedness in subjects with high narcissism, resulting in decreased spatial and temporal continuity. Together, this supports a spatio-temporal view of both self and narcissism where topography and dynamic are shared as "common currency" by neuronal and psychological levels.

References

Babo-Rebelo M, Buot A, Tallon-Baudry C (2019) Neural responses to heartbeats distinguish self from other during imagination. NeuroImage. 191:10–20. doi: 10.1016/j.neuroimage.2019.02.012

Babo-Rebelo M, Wolpert N, Adam C, Hasboun D, Tallon-Baudry C (2016) Is the cardiac monitoring function related to the self in both the default network and right anterior insula? Philos. Trans. R. Soc. Lond. B. Biol. Sci. 371:20160004. doi: 10.1098/rstb.2016.0004

Buzsaki G (2006) Rhythms of the brain. Oxford University Press, Oxford. doi: 10.1093/acprof:oso/9780195301069.001.0001

Chester DS, DeWall CN (2016) Sound the alarm: The effect of narcissism on retaliatory aggression is moderated by dACC reactivity to rejection. J Pers. Jun;84(3):361–368. doi: 10.1111/jopy.12164. Epub 2015 Feb 17.

Chester DS, Lynam DR, Powell DK, DeWall CN (2016) Narcissism is associated with weakened frontostriatal connectivity: A DTI study. Soc Cogn Affect Neurosci. 2016 Jul;11(7):1036–1040. doi: 10.1093/scan/nsv069. Epub 2015 Jun 5.

Craig AD (2003) Interoception: The sense of the physiological condition of the body. Curr. Opin. Neurobiol. 13:500–505. doi: 10.1016/s0959-4388(03)00090-4

Craig AD (2010) The sentient self. Brain Struct. Funct. 214:563–577. doi: 10.1007/s00429-010-0248-y

Damasio A (2010) Self comes to mind: Constructing the conscious brain. Pantheon Books, New York.

Fan Y, Wonneberger C, Enzi B, de Greck M, Ulrich C, Tempelmann C, Bogerts B, Doering S, Northoff G (2011) The narcissistic self and its psychological and neural correlates: An exploratory fMRI study. Psychol Med. Aug;41(8):1641–1650. doi: 10.1017/S003329171000228X. Epub 2010 Dec 13.

Feng C, Yuan J, Geng H, Gu R, Zhou H, Wu X, Luo Y (2018) Individualized prediction of trait narcissism from whole-brain resting-state functional connectivity. Hum Brain Mapp. Sep;39(9):3701–3712. doi: 10.1002/hbm.24205. Epub 2018 May 10.

Frewen P, Schroeter ML, Riva G, Cipresso P, Fairfield B, Padulo C, Kemp AH, Palaniyappan L, Owolabi M, Kusi-Mensah K, Polyakova M, Fehertoi N, D'Andrea W, Lowe L, Northoff G (2020) Neuroimaging the consciousness of self: Review, and conceptual-methodological framework. Neurosci Biobehav Rev. May;112:164–212. doi: 10.1016/j.neubiorev.2020.01.023. Epub 2020 Jan 26. PMID: 31996300 Free article. Review.

Gallagher S (2005) Dynamic models of body schematic processes. Adv. Consc. Res. 62:233–250. doi: 10.1075/aicr.62.15gal

Gehrie MJ (2009) The evolution of the psychology of the self: Towards a mature narcissism. Annals New York Academy of Sciences. 1159:31–50.

Hasson U, Chen J, Honey CJ (2015) Hierarchical process memory: Memory as an integral component of information processing. Trends Cogn. Sci. 19(6):304–313. doi: 10.1016/j.tics.2015.04.006

He BJ (2014) Scale-free brain activity: Past, present, and future. Trends Cogn. Sci. 18:480–487. doi: 10.1016/j.tics.2014.04.003

He BJ, Zempel JM, Snyder AZ, Raichle ME (2010) The temporal structures and functional significance of scale-free brain activity. Neuron. 66:353–369. doi: 10.1016/j.neuron.2010.04.020

Huang Z, Obara N, Davis HH 4th, Pokorny J, Northoff G (2016) The temporal structure of resting-state brain activity in the medial prefrontal cortex predicts self-consciousness. Neuropsychologia. 82:161–170. doi: 10.1016/j. neuropsychologia.2016.01.025

Jauk E, Benedek M, Koschutnig K, Kedia G, Neubauer AC (2017) Self-viewing is associated with negative affect rather than reward in highly narcissistic men: An fMRI study. Sci Rep. Jul 19;7(1):5804. doi: 10.1038/s41598-017-03935-y

Kernberg OF (1984) Severe personality disorders: Psychotherapeutic strategies. Yale University Press, New Haven.

Kohut H (1977) The restoration of the self. Int Universities Press, New York.

Kohut H (1984) How does analysis cure? Chicago University Press, Chicago.

Kolvoort IR, Wainio-Theberge S, Wolff A, Northoff G (2020) Temporal integration as "common currency" of brain and self-scale-free activity in resting-state EEG correlates with temporal delay effects on self-relatedness. Hum. Brain Mapp. 41:4355–4374. doi: 10.1002/hbm.25129

Linkenkaer-Hansen K, Nikouline VV, Palva JM, Ilmoniemi RJ (2001) Long-range temporal correlations and scaling behavior in human brain oscillations. J. Neurosci. 21:1370–1377. doi: 10.1523/JNEUROSCI.21-04-01370.2001

Lou J, Sun Y, Cui Z, Gong L (2021) Structural brain alterations in young adult males with narcissistic personality disorder: A diffusion tensor imaging study. Int J Neurosci. Mar 8:1–8. doi: 10.1080/00207454.2021.1896504. Online ahead of print.

Mao Y, Sang N, Wang Y, Hou X, Huang H, Wei D, Zhang J, Qiu J (2016) Reduced frontal cortex thickness and cortical volume associated with pathological narcissism. Neuroscience. Jul 22;328:50–57. doi: 10.1016/j.neuroscience.2016.04.025. Epub 2016 Apr 27. PMID: 27129440.

Menon V (2011) Large-scale brain networks and psychopathology: A unifying triple network model. Trends Cogn. Sci. 15:483–506. doi: 10.1016/j.tics.2011.08.003

Milrod D (2002) The concept of self and the self representation. Neuropsychoanalysis. 4(1):7–23.

Nenadic I, Güllmar D, Dietzek M, Langbein K, Steinke J, Gaser C. (2015) Brain structure in narcissistic personality disorder: A VBM and DTI pilot study. Psychiatry Res. Feb 28;231(2):184–186. doi: 10.1016/j.pscychresns.2014.11.001. Epub 2014 Nov 8.

Northoff G (2016) Is the self a higher-order or fundamental function of the brain? The "basis model of self-specificity" and its encoding by the brain's spontaneous activity. Cogn. Neurosci. 7(1–4):203–222. doi: 10.1080/17588928.2015.1111868

Northoff G (2017) Personal identity and cortical midline structure (CMS): Do temporal features of CMS neural activity transform into "self-continuity"?. Psychol. Inq. 28(2–3):122–131. doi: 10.1080/1047840X.2017.1337396

Northoff G, Huang Z (2017) How do the brain's time and space mediate consciousness and its different dimensions? Temporo-spatial theory of consciousness (TTC). Neurosci. Biobehav. Rev. 80:630–645. doi: 10.1016/j.neubiorev.2017.07.013

Northoff G, Qin P, Feinberg TE (2011) Brain imaging of the self: Conceptual, anatomical and methodological issues. Conscious Cogn. Mar;20(1):52–63. doi: 10.1016/j.concog.2010.09.011. Epub 2010 Oct 6.

Northoff G, Wainio-Theberge S, Evers K (2020a) Is temporo-spatial dynamics the "common currency" of brain and mind? In quest of "spatiotemporal neuroscience". Phys Life Rev. 33:34–54. doi: 10.1016/j.plrev.2019.05.002

Northoff G, Wainio-Theberge S, Evers K (2020b). Spatiotemporal neuroscience – What is it and why we need it. Phys Life Rev. 33:78–87. doi: 10.1016/j.plrev.2020.06.005

Northoff G, Wiebking C, Feinberg T, Panksepp J (2011) The "resting-state hypothesis" of major depressive disorder-a translational subcortical-cortical framework for a system disorder. Neurosci Biobehav Rev. Oct;35(9):1929–1945. doi: 10.1016/j.neubiorev.2010.12.007. Epub 2010 Dec 28.

Panksepp J (1998) The periconscious substrates of consciousness: Affective states and the evolutionary origins of the self. J. Conscious. Stud. 5:566–582.

Panksepp J (2012) What is an emotional feeling? Lessons about affective origins from cross-species neuroscience. Motiv. Emot. 36:4–15. doi: 10.1007/s11031-011-9232-y

Qin P, Wang M, Northoff G (2020) Linking bodily, environmental and mental states in the self—A three-level model based on a meta-analysis. Neurosci Biobehav Rev. 115:77–95. doi: 10.1016/j.neubiorev. 2020.05.004

Scalabrini A, Ebisch SJH, Huang Z, Di Plinio S, Perrucci MG, Romani GL, et al (2019) Spontaneous brain activity predicts task-evoked activity during animate versus inanimate touch. Cereb Cortex 29:4628–4645. doi: 10.1093/cercor/bhy340

Scalabrini A, Huang Z, Mucci C, Perrucci MG, Ferretti A, Fossati A, Romani GL, Northoff G, Ebisch SJH (2017) How spontaneous brain activity and narcissistic features shape social interaction. Sci Rep. Aug 30;7(1):9986. doi: 10.1038/s41598-017-10389-9

Sui J, Humphreys GW (2015) The integrative self: How self-reference integrates perception and memory. Trends Cogn Sci. Dec;19(12):719–728. doi: 10.1016/j.tics.2015.08.015. Epub 2015 Oct 4.

Tsakiris M (2017) The multisensory basis of the self: From body to identity to others. Q. J. Exp. Psychol. (Hove). 70:597–609. doi: 10.1080/17470218.2016.1181768

Wiest G (2012) Neural and mental hierarchies. Front Psychol. Nov 26;3:516. doi: 10.3389/fpsyg.2012.00516. eCollection 2012.

Wolff A, Di Giovanni DA, Gómez-Pilar J, Nakao T, Huang Z, Longtin A, Northoff G (2019) The temporal signature of self: Temporal measures of resting-state EEG predict self-consciousness. Hum Brain Mapp. Feb 15;40(3):789–803. doi: 10.1002/hbm.24412. Epub 2018 Oct 4.

Chapter 2

Attachment and trauma

Introduction

We characterized the topography of the brain-based self in the previous chapter. This let us distinguish three different layers of self, interoceptive, exteroceptive, and mental-cognitive. While detailing the relationship of brain and self, we more or less neglected the context within which the brain-based self operates, namely body and environment. The relationship of self to its environment is key, especially in psychoanalysis, where it is thematized in terms of attachment and trauma.

There is abundant literature on both attachment and trauma in current psychoanalysis, including their connection to body and brain. Rather than discussing all the details of that, we here focus on their deeper dimensions, namely their spatial topography and temporal dynamic, which, in turn, render the kind of affective and cognitive features emphasized in the literature. Highlighting the brain's spatiotemporal relationship to body and world, our focus is on the inter-subjective and ultimately neuro-ecological/social dimension of both attachment and trauma rather than on their intra-subjective features like vegetative, affective, and cognitive symptoms.

DOI: 10.4324/9781003132905-3

Part I: attachment – topographic and dynamic view

The scale-free world – nature and world exhibit scale-free temporal structure

We already encountered scale-free activity in the brain, the long-range temporal correlations between slow/long and fast/short timescales (Chapter 1). Most interestingly, similar LRTC can be observed within the natural world in a ubiquitous way. What do the brain, weather, seismic waves, and stock markets have in common? Prima facie, you will insist that they are unrelated; the brain is a lump of gray matter consisting of neurons, which, of course, cannot be observed in the others. However, fluctuations in the activity of, for instance, seismic earth waves exhibit the same scale-free structure characterized by temporal nestedness with LRTC as the brain. Hence, one of the most interesting aspects of scale-free activity is its universality.

Scale-free activity is not unique to the brain; rather, it is ubiquitous in nature, evident across systems as varied as climate, seismic activity, magnetic fields, and stock markets (Cocchi et al. 2017; He et al. 2010). Basically, wherever irregular fluctuations in activity are observed, LRTC and scale-free activity may provide structure to what initially appears to be random noise. There is "structure to irregularity", and that seems to be a unifying principle and key feature of nature and the world in general.

For instance, He et al. (2010) investigated the scale-free dynamics of the brain's neural activity and its nested frequencies using intracranial EEG, that is, ECoG. In addition, they investigated the time series of spontaneous seismic activity (collected within a timespan of 4 months) and fluctuations in the Dow-Jones index (collected over a period of 80 years). Time series from both seismic waves and stock market fluctuations followed a power-law distribution in their temporal power spectrum. Interestingly, their power-law exponents (1.99 for seismic waves and 1.95 for the stock market) resembled that of the brain's intrinsic activity measured in ECoG during wakefulness (mean of 2.2 for <0.1 hz). Of further significance, like the brain's intrinsic activity, the time series of both seismic waves and stock market fluctuations contained nested frequencies (that is, higher-frequency fluctuations nesting in lower-frequency fluctuations). Together, these and various other findings show that scale-free nestedness is prevalent not only in the brain but ubiquitous in nature and thus the world.

Self and world I – LRTCs match and connect brain and world

How are the world's scale-free features related to those of the brain? Given that the world shapes the brain through traumatic life events (see subsequently), one would expect a close relationship, if not an interaction, between their respective scale-free features. Specifically, one would predict that the LRTCs of the environmental structures contain and nest those of the brain's spontaneous activity – both ecological and neuronal LRTC would be expected to match across (and despite) their different time scales. Such "scale-free complexity matching" (West et al. 2008) through the nestedness of the brain's LRTC within the world's LRTC has indeed been shown in recent studies on language and music.

Borges et al. (2018), for instance, demonstrated how the degree of scale-freeness in the brain in different frequency bands follows the variations in the scale-free envelope of speech and how their degree of correspondence impacts speech comprehension. Analogously, Borges et al. (2019) show how the scale-free structures of the brain and music adapt to each other, with the brain's neural activity somewhat rescaling the musical structure. The timing of the neuronal fluctuations, as observed in the brain's scale-free activity, followed the timing of the fluctuations in the music (i.e., its scale-free activity), although the latter operated on a wider range of temporal scales than the brain. Moreover, the scale-free adaptation of subjects' neural activity to the music predicted their degree of pleasure.

Together, these findings show that the degree of matching or concordance of the scale-free properties in the environmental context (i.e., language or music in our case) and brain strongly shape one's mental features like the feeling of pleasure and the sense of self. This suggests a truly neuro-ecological basis of our self and its intrinsic subjectivity within the world, mediated by the temporal nestedness of the brain within the world, the world–brain relation (Northoff 2018).

Self and world II – LRTCs of the brain nest the self within the world

How are the self and its neural basis in the brain related to the scale-free activity in the world? Scalabrini et al. (2019) investigated the relationship of the self to animate and inanimate contexts as operationalized by a real person's hand vs an artificial mechanical hand, respectively. He showed that, on a purely psychological level, subjects perceived the real hand as more self-specific, closer to the own self in subjective space, and more temporally synchronous with the own self. This suggests that animate and inanimate features like the real vs artificial hand are perceived on the psychological level in distinct ways in terms of their self, time, and space. We are thus connected and attached more intimately to the real hand than the artificial one.

In a second step, he conducted fMRI, exposing subjects again to both hands, real and artificial. He demonstrated that the scale-free activity of the brain's resting state activity (as measured by the power law exponent) in the medial prefrontal cortex is related to the degree to which task-related activity differs between real and artificial hands, that is, animate and inanimate contexts: the higher the PLE in the resting state, the stronger the distinction between animate and inanimate context during task-related activity. Accordingly, the brain's scale-free activity connects its own scale-free features, as mediating the self, to environmental contexts like the animate hand.

Given the fact that the brain's scale-freeness is directly related to the self, it is a logical assumption that the self is connected and integrated within the world's scale-free structure through temporal nestedness and LRTC. Analogous to how the smallest Russian doll is integrated within the next larger one and so forth, the self is integrated and nested within the brain, which, in turn, is nested and integrated within the world, providing the largest and most comprehensive and integrative temporal scale.

Accordingly, what connects the self through the brain to the world is its scale-freeness featuring temporal nestedness and LRTC. Conceived from the point of view of the world itself, the brain and its various timescales are just one instance through which the world's timescales are realized in a scale-free way with LRTC. Scale-free activity thus constitutes an intimate scale-free temporal relation of world and brain as featured by their LRTCs.

In sum, we can say that: (i) the world–brain relation is scale-free and characterized by temporal nestedness and LRTC, implying that the world's larger scale nests and contains the brain's smaller scales; (ii) the scale-free nature of the world–brain relation may be critical in shaping and constituting the self; (iii) this entails that the self is intrinsically neuro-ecological and temporal, that is, scale-free, meaning that (iv) the self is intrinsically integrated within the world through its temporal nestedness and LRTC.

Attachment I – temporal continuity of self and world

We see that the self is not a monolithic entity but a structure that spans the internal–external divide of brain, body, and world. This internal–external structure is based on a nested hierarchy across the boundaries of brain, body, and world in both space and time that translates into a more or less corresponding temporo-spatially nested hierarchy of self. As such, the key connection of self and world is constituted by the structure of time, namely the degree of scale-free-ness and temporal nestedness of the brain-based self within body and world. Since scale-freeness constitutes LRTC and thus temporal continuity, the self can be characterized by a temporally continuous relationship with body and world – the self is intrinsically relational.

We now assume that such a scale-free temporal continuity of self, body, and world is key in mediating what is described as attachment in current psychology and psychoanalysis. Attachment to others and, more generally, the world, is the most basic and fundamental mechanism by which the self constitutes itself and maintains its temporal continuity and stability. At the same time, such attachment also allows the self adapting to changing contexts that introduce temporal discontinuity and require temporal flexibility.

Taken together, attachment is here conceived in primarily temporal terms as based on the temporal continuity and nestedness of the self to and within its ecological and social environment. This, as we assume, provides the fundament for the more affective and cognitive features of attachment that are highlighted in psychology and psychoanalysis. We thus complement the affective and cognitive views of attachment by a deeper temporal and dynamic layer that, as we assume, drives and constitutes the former.

Attachment II – attachment is neuro-ecological/ social, temporal, and scale free

Let us sketch the need for temporal continuity by example of mother and infant. One of the key features the mother needs to provide for the infant is temporal continuity, the continuous presence of the mother, including the continuous presence of its more or less stable affective-emotional relationship to the infant. Neuronally, this may be manifest in the lacking integration of the infant's interoceptive input with the mother's exteroceptive inputs, while psychologically this leads to decreased attachment and, in extreme cases, to trauma (see subsequently).

If that temporal continuity of the mother's physical, affective, and mental presence is disrupted or even abolished (by, for instance, the death of the mother), the infant's nestedness within its mother's relationship (and ultimately the world) cannot be properly established. This is like taking one or two dolls out of the whole set of Russian dolls: the infant's self and its different layers cannot be integrated within a larger relational neuro-social context anymore. In the same way that the continuity of the Russian dolls is affected when taking one or two more dolls out, the temporal continuity of self and environment is disrupted by the mother's physical and/or mental absence.

Accordingly, disruption of the inter-subjective attachment of mother and infant ultimately disrupts the nestedness of the infant's self itself with its social and ecological environmental context. Attachment is thus understood in a relational, that is neuro-ecological and neuro-social, way. Such a fundamental view of attachment as neuro-ecological/social, temporal, and nested is well in line with its psychodynamic determination by Brockman: "Attachment begins before any sense of self and before any sense of object to attach to. . . . Attachment begins before emotions, and indeed belongs to a different biological system than emotions" (Brokman 2002, 90). We complement this by assuming that the concepts of "before emotions", "before any sense of self", and "different biological system" can be related to and specified by the topography and dynamic of the brain's scale-free spatiotemporal nestedness within the world.

In sum, we here advocate a spatiotemporal view of attachment in terms of a nested world–brain/self relation. Importantly, such a spatiotemporal view does not exclude cognitive and affective characterizations of attachment. Instead it provides a more comprehensive and broader context through which attachment and ultimately also the self are intrinsically integrated and embedded within the world. This also aligns more or less well with the various more relational and inter-subjective psychodynamic conceptions of self or ego as proposed by Freud, Kohut, Winnicott, Stern, Milrod, Fonagy, Solms, and Panksepp/Biven (and many others).

Part II: trauma – topographic and dynamic view

We demonstrated that intimate spatiotemporal nestedness of the self within the world through scale-freeness and LRTC allows constituting attachment. However, the spatiotemporal attachment of the self within the world comes at a price. This spatial and temporal continuity interweaving the brain-based self within the world may be disrupted by external life events. If those life events disrupt the self, one may speak of trauma. Here, following the topography of self with its three layers, we assume corresponding layers of trauma. For that, we follow the excellent account of trauma by the Italian psychoanalyst Clara Mucci's interdisciplinary and clinical observation (2013, 2018), which, in part, relies on Alan Schore (2003): she distinguishes between three layers of inter-personal trauma that we, in a second step, connect with the different layers of self in its nested neural hierarchy.

Mucci (2013, 2018) distinguishes between three levels of inter-personal trauma that reflect different degrees in the severity of disrupted attachment across the life span from infancy to adulthood. Notably, all three levels of trauma are not separated entities but rather refer to different degrees of an underlying continuum of trauma severity and depth. Hence, the distinction of the three levels of trauma is more heuristic and conceptual; they should not be confused with the actual reality itself, where one can observe multiple transitions and overlaps with possible cumulative effects and influences between one level and the other.

First layer of trauma I – early relational trauma, subcortical–cortical limbic regions and the interoceptive self

The first, most basic level of inter-personal trauma concerns what Mucci (2013, 2018) and Schore (2003) describe as "early relational trauma". This mostly goes back to early infancy where the infant suffers from a lack of attachment by the caregiver who is unable to provide secure, stable, and continuous care and containment for the infant (Schore 2003). Such a lack of attachment may be related to various forms of mother–infant relationship: the mother may be physically present but mentally absent; she may also be physically absent, or taking care of the infant but in an emotionally cold way (or various other constellations). Hence, there is a lack of the most basic attunement of mother and infant, which induces relational trauma in the latter.

Characteristic of this first layer of trauma is that the most basic physiological and subsequently psychological needs of the infant for developing attachment are not met at all. This creates disorganized attachment (Liotti 1992) in the infant and makes it prone to most basic dissociative responses (Mucci 2018; Mucci and Scalabrini 2021; Scalabrini et al. 2020) in childhood and later adulthood. Moreover, the infant or child suffers from affective dysregulation with hypoarousal, which later may translate into high vulnerability to depression, anxiety, and the development of trauma-related personality disorders.

Neuronally, such early relational trauma has been associated with changes in various cortical and subcortical brain regions that belong to the limbic system, including the insula and the orbitofrontal cortex (Schore 2003). Interestingly, these regions strongly overlap with those recruited during the most basic layer of self in the nested neural hierarchy, the interoceptive self: subcortical regions like the thalamus and those in the midbrain and even brain stem as well as cortical regions like the insula mediate the most basic layer of the interoceptive self, including how it connects to the exteroceptive inputs from the environment (see Chapter 1).

These subcortical–cortical regions predominantly process and integrate interoceptive stimuli and inputs from the subject's own inner body and, in later stages, their integration with exteroceptive inputs. This is the most fundamental layer of the self, which ties it closely to the own body and environment, that is, the most basic intero- and exteroceptive inputs, any infant (and later child and adult) receives. Disturbances in these regions' interoceptive processing consequently lead to major disturbances in the most basic sense of self, that is, the interoceptive self. How does that translate into the symptoms of trauma? That shall be discussed in the next section.

First layer of trauma II – from irregular/absent interoceptive input to disordered attachment

How is this most basic and fundamental layer of the interoceptive self related to the symptoms of early relational trauma? If the caregiver like the mother does not provide proper care like nutrition in a regular and predictable way, the interoceptive inputs to the subcortical regions and the insula are highly irregular and/or absent. What is described as "disorganized attachment" on the psychological level (Mucci 2013, 2018; Schore 2003) may then be related to "disorganized interoceptive input" on the level of the brain's intero-exteroceptive input processing: irregular or even absent intero-exteroceptive inputs from the mother to the infant will make it rather difficult for the latter's interoceptive processing, especially in its limbic subcortical and cortical regions, to develop a proper dynamic, that is, a power spectrum with a balance of slow and fast frequencies in a scale-free and temporally well-integrated and nested way.

Specifically, there may be a disbalance of slow and fast frequencies that, in turn, impedes all subsequent processing in the limbic subcortical regions, including their integration of the various interoceptive (and later also exteroceptive) inputs on the more cortical level in, for instance, the insula. If, however, intero-intero/exteroceptive integration in subcortical regions and insula (and other cortical regions) is impaired, the infant's sense of its interoceptive self may become disorganized and thereby unstable and fragile – the self of those subjects shows a lack of energy, with hypoarousal (as eventually related to the nucleus basalis of Meynert), affective dysregulation (as eventually related to serotoninergic and adrenergic/norardrenergic subcortical regions; Panksepp and Biven 2012), and lack of bodily memory and dissociation proneness (as related to the lack of intero- and exteroceptive integration and decreased connectivity of the insula; Scalabrini et al. 2019, 2020).

Together, irregular or absent intero-exteroceptive inputs through the caregiver may translate into corresponding neuronal topographic subcortical–cortical disbalances and dynamic slow–fast irregularities in the dynamics of their power spectrum. The subcortical–cortical regions' abnormally slow–fast balanced power spectrum with decreased temporal nestedness, in turn, may be related to decreased arousal, affective dysregulation, and an unstable or fragile interoceptive self. Such "disorganized topography and dynamic" of the brain's most basic subcortical–cortical layer of the interoceptive self may be manifest in what has been described as "disorganized attachment" on the psychological level (Mucci 2013, 2018, 2019).

Second layer of trauma I – from maltreatment and abuse to the dissociation of self

The second level of inter-personal trauma concerns what Mucci (2013, 2018, 2019) describe as "maltreatment and abuse". This refers to those kinds of events that often exceed the "normal" ranges of human experience, like maltreatment, severe emotional and physical deprivation, and incest and abuse.

These events can occur at every time of the life cycle, including in infancy or early childhood, where they may have major reverberations for the psyche. As emphasized here, these events may mainly occur in infancy and early childhood, where they leave major consequences for later adulthood. Dissociation and/or identification with the aggressor characterize this second level of trauma described by Mucci (2013, 2018). This implies relation to the other person that distinguishes this second level of trauma from the first level, where no such relation by itself and subsequently no attachment as such is constituted.

How is that related to the nested hierarchy of self? The second layer of the nested hierarchy extends beyond the interoceptive self to the extero-proprioceptive self that features the processing of proprio-exteroceptive input from the outside of one's own body and others' relative to the own body. This is neuronally reflected in the recruitment of regions like the anterior medial prefrontal cortex, premotor, fusiform face area, and temporo-parietal junction that typically process these kinds of inputs (see Qin et al. 2020). Importantly, this proprio-exteroceptive layer of self builds and nests upon the more fundamental first layer, the interoceptive input layer of self: the latter and its regions are integrated within the former. Such a nested hierarchical relationship carries major implications for how trauma affects the self and how the self can cope with trauma.

Second layer of trauma II – topographic-dynamic reorganization of the traumatized proprio-exteroceptive self

One may now postulate that the second level of trauma, with abuse, maltreatment, and/or physical and emotional deprivation, may primarily affect the extero-proprioceptive layer of the self by disrupting the activity of its respective regions. The extero-proprioceptive layer of self may be taken out and split off from the nested hierarchy, including its containment or nesting within the interoceptive layer of self – this is like "taking out" one of the more intermediate-sized Russian dolls, which then, relatively speaking, will enlarge the next lower one in a disproportionate way. Neural activity will thus "fall back" onto the more basic and fundamental layer, the interoceptive input layer. That may, for instance, be manifest in abnormally strong manifestation of interoceptive awareness and the interoceptive self in subjects suffering from second-layer trauma – extreme anxiety, insecurity, and dissociation (negative symptoms) are typical manifestations.

We need to be more careful, though. The traumatized layer is not completely "taken out". The predominantly traumatized layer is still present, but it shrinks relative to the next lower layer, the interoceptive layer of self. This results in an abnormal disbalance between intero- and exteroceptive layers: the former predominates over the latter in traumatized individuals, whereas in healthy subjects, the exteroceptive layer dominates the interoceptive layer by integrating and embedding it in a larger-scale temporal and spatial context.

Psychologically, this means that the extero-proprioceptive self may become abnormally small, shrink, and no longer be visible within the more overarching interoceptive layer of self. Put in spatiotemporal terms, this means that the spatial extension and the temporal range of the extero-proprioceptive self may be reduced to the ultimately smaller spatial and temporal ranges of the interoceptive self. Rather than being directed outwards to the exteroceptive world, the self in these subjects is more focused on the own inner interoceptive body, resulting in enhanced awareness and sensitivity to interoceptive changes and consequently heightened arousal and enhanced anxiety (Mucci 2018; Schore 2003). This propels us to shed some brief light on the consequences of trauma, the person's reaction.

How can the person defend its own self and react to its decreased temporo-spatial nestedness of its different layers of self? It may try to "fill in" the "missing" second extero-proprioceptive layer of self: this may be possible through either interoceptive strengthening (as the first layer of self) and/or mental or cognitive efforts (as the third layer of self), like identification with aggressor (as theorized by Mucci 2013, 2018). That, as we say, reflects the reorganization of (i) the spatial topography of the nested neural hierarchy of self and (ii) the temporal dynamic with its slow–fast balance of the power spectrum. We will see in the next chapter that such a topographic-dynamic reorganization in response to trauma leads us to defense mechanisms, including dissociation as one of the key symptoms.

Third layer of trauma – topographic-dynamic reorganization of the traumatized mental or cognitive self

Even during adolescence or adulthood, we may experience major trauma with events like genocide, war, and rape/abuse (or intergenerational trauma) that lie outside the "normal" range of human experiences. How do brain and self react to that? This depends, in part, on the time of the traumatic occurrence: the same trauma may have different impacts depending on whether it occurs during infancy, adolescence, or adulthood, as these are related to the different layers of the nested hierarchy of self. Moreover, it depends upon the severity of trauma: the more severe a trauma, the more strongly it will reverberate into the deeper layers of self.

One may assume that traumata primarily affect the most upper surface layer of self, the mental or cognitive self, and its underlying regions like the cortical midline structures. Neural activity in these regions may be diminished and reduced in the face of such severe trauma, which is indeed supported by various results (see Mucci 2013, 2018, 2019; Mucci and Scalabrini 2021 for overviews). The mental self, as the uppermost layer of the self, is consequently diminished. This means that the self's role as psychological baseline or default mode for the brain's mental features (Northoff et al. 2022; Scalabrini et al. 2021) is put "out of order".

That changes the whole nested hierarchy of self. The uppermost layer, the mental self, is now abnormally "shrunk", which, relatively speaking, renders the interoceptive and extero-proprioceptive layers of self abnormally strong (in relative and/or absolute terms). This is, for instance, reflected in the often observed increases of anxiety and interoceptive awareness in these subjects who also suffer from depression, anxiety disorder, and trauma-related personality disorders (Mucci 2013, 2018; Mucci and Scalabrini 2021).

At the same time, the mental or cognitive features of the self may be "split" from its lower nesting layers, the intero- and extero-proprioceptive layers of self. That may be reflected in the various compartmentalization and detachment symptoms of dissociation, for example, positive symptoms (see Chapter 3 for details) (Scalabrini et al. 2020). Dissociation may here thus be understood as the disruption of the "glue" or spatiotemporal nestedness between the different layers of self – this, as we postulate, may be traced to a corresponding disruption in the spatial and temporal nestedness among the neural layers of self.

Accordingly, what is described as dissociation of parts of the self on the psychological level may be mediated by a corresponding dissociation on the neural level of self: the DMN mediating the mental or cognitive layer of self dissociates from its nesting neural layers, the subcortical–cortical layers of both the interoceptive and extero-proprioceptive self. Correspondingly, the nestedness of the DMN's dynamics of the power spectrum will dissociate from the slow–fast dynamics of the regions mediating the interoceptive and proprio-exteroceptive layers of self. This results in the disruption of the temporo-spatial nestedness of the brain's hierarchical topography and dynamics with abnormal disbalances both among the three spatial layers and their slow–fast dynamics. The third level of trauma (and trauma in general) can thus be characterized by disintegration or dissociation between the different temporo-spatial layers of the hierarchy of self. I assume that such neuronal-hierarchical dissociation results in corresponding dissociation on the psychological level – this is manifest in the three layers of trauma.

Conclusion

We discussed two key features of current psychoanalysis, namely attachment and trauma, in the context of the brain and its spatiotemporal characterization. This revealed a deeper layer of attachment beyond sensory, affective, and cognitive functions. Attachment is here determined by the spatial topography and temporal dynamic of how the brain is connected to its environmental context, the world. This amounts to a neuro-ecological/social and temporally nested scale-free integration of the brain-based self within body and world. While this makes the self optimally adaptive to the world, at the same time, it renders it vulnerable to disrupting life-events within that very same world. That is manifest in what is described as trauma.

Following the topography and dynamic of the brain-based self (Chapter 1), as well as recent psychodynamic assumption of three-layer trauma (by Alan Shore and Clara Mucci), we distinguish three layers of trauma on both neural and psychological grounds. These are the (i) interoceptive level of trauma as related to lack of mother-infant attachment/attunement; (ii) proprio-exteroceptive level of trauma due to maltreatment, abuse, and incest; and (iii) mental-cognitive level of trauma, with massive trauma, including intergenerational trauma.

In conclusion, we converge the three-layer neuro-hierarchical model of self with three levels of attachment and trauma through their corresponding spatial-topographic and temporal-dynamic features. This is made possible by the fact that topography and dynamic are shared by all three brain/body, self, and environment/world as their "common currency". Since that provides the basis for attachment, our relation to others is stabilizing for the self through constituting its spatial and temporal continuity with the world. At the same time, lack or disruption of the self's attachment to others and the world at its different layers (interceptive, proprio-exteroceptive, mental-cognitive) can disrupt its spatial and temporal continuity with the world, resulting in trauma.

References

Borges A, Irrmischer M, Brockmeier T, Smit DJA, Mansvelder HD, Linkenkaer-Hansen K (2019) Scaling behaviour in music and cortical dynamics interplay to mediate music listening pleasure. Scientific Report. Nov 27;9(1):17700. doi: 10.1038/s41598-019-54060-x

Borges AFT, Giraud AL, Mansvelder HD, Linkenkaer-Hansen K (2018) Scale-free amplitude modulation of neuronal oscillations tracks comprehension of accelerated speech. J Neurosci. Jan 17;38(3):710–722. doi: 10.1523/JNEUROSCI.1515-17.2017. Epub 2017 Dec 7.

Brockman R (2002) Self, object, and neurobiology. Neuropsychoanalysis. 4:87–99.

Cocchi L, Gollo LL, Zalesky A, Breakspear M (2017) Criticality in the brain: A synthesis of neurobiology, models and cognition. Prog Neurobiol. Nov;158:132–152. doi: 10.1016/j.pneurobio.2017.07.002. Epub 2017 Jul 19. PMID: 28734836 Review.

He BJ, Zempel JM, Snyder AZ, Raichle ME (2010) The temporal structures and functional significance of scale-free brain activity. Neuron. May 13;66(3):353–369. doi: 10.1016/j.neuron.2010.04.020

Liotti G (1992) Disorganized/disoriented attachment in the etiology of the dissociative disorders. Dissociation: Progress in the Dissociative Disorders. 5(4):196–204.

Mucci C (2013) Beyond individual and collective trauma: Intergenerational transmission, psychoanalytic treatment, and the dynamics of forgiveness. Routledge, Abingdon, UK.

Mucci C (2018) Borderline bodies: Affect regulation therapy for personality disorders (Norton Series on Interpersonal Neurobiology). WW Norton & Company, New York.

Mucci C (2019) Traumatization through human agency: "Embodied witnessing" is essential in the treatment of survivors. Am. J. Psychoanal. 79:540–554. doi: 10.1057/s11231-019-09225-y

Mucci C, Scalabrini A (2021) Traumatic effects beyond diagnosis: The impact of dissociation on the mind-body-brain system. Psychoanal. Psychol. doi: 10.1037/pap0000332

Northoff G (2018) The spontaneous brain: From the mind-body to the world-brain relation. MIT Press, Cambridge, MA.

Northoff G, Vatansever D, Scalabrini A, Stamatakis EA (2022) Ongoing brain activity and its role in cognition: Dual versus baseline models. Neuroscientist. May 25:10738584221081752. doi: 10.1177/10738584221081752. Online ahead of print

Panksepp J, Biven L (2012) The archaeology of mind: Neuroevolutionary origins of human emotions (Norton Series on Interpersonal Neurobiology). WW Norton & Company, New York.

Qin P, Wang M, Northoff G (2020) Linking bodily, environmental and mental states in the self-A three-level model based on a meta-analysis. Neurosci Biobehav Rev. Aug;115:77–95. doi: 10.1016/j.neubiorev.2020.05.004. Epub 2020 May 31.

Scalabrini A, Ebisch SJH, Huang Z, Di Plinio S, Perrucci MG, Romani GL, Mucci C, Northoff G (2019) Spontaneous brain activity predicts task-evoked activity during animate versus inanimate touch. Cereb Cortex. Dec 17;29(11):4628–4645. doi: 10.1093/cercor/bhy340

Scalabrini A, Esposito R, Mucci C (2021) Dreaming the unrepressed unconscious and beyond: Repression vs dissociation in the oneiric functioning of severe patients. Res Psychother. Aug 12;24(2):545. doi: 10.4081/ripppo.2021.545. eCollection 2021 Aug 12.

Scalabrini A, Mucci C, Esposito R, Damiani S, Northoff G (2020) Dissociation as a disorder of integration: On the footsteps of Pierre Janet. Prog Neuropsychopharmacol Biol Psychiatry. Jul 13;101:109928. doi: 10.1016/j.pnpbp.2020.109928

Schore AN (2003) Affect dysregulation and disorders of the self (Norton Series on Interpersonal Neurobiology). WW Norton & Company, New York.

West BJ, Geneston EL, Grigolini P (2008) Maximizing information exchange between complex networks. Phys Rep. 468:1–99. doi: 10.1016/j. physrep.2008.06.003

Chapter 3

Defense mechanisms and dissociation

Introduction

Defense mechanisms I – topographic and dynamic reorganization of the self

Trauma can be detrimental to the self, as it disrupts the nested neural and psychological hierarchies of self, as we have seen in the last chapter. The self can defend itself against such trauma, though. This leads us to what has been described psychodynamically as defense mechanisms. The body has its own physiological defense mechanisms, namely the immune system that allows the body to defend itself against foreign intruders like viruses by producing its own antibodies. Defense mechanisms of the psyche are here understood in a more or less analogous and thus biological way; the main difference is that defense mechanisms do not concern the body but the self that is defended against foreign intrusions and threats.

What are defense mechanisms, and what is their purpose? Roughly, defense mechanisms are a set of diverse psychic or mental mechanisms that the self can recruit in response to conflict resulting from either external traumatic events or internal contradictory thoughts, memories, and/or emotions. The purpose of defense mechanisms is to keep the self and, more generally, the psyche stable and continuous in order to protect them from the instabilities and discontinuities of both the internal and external environment. Psychologically, instabilities and discontinuities lead to anxiety and insecurity against which the self has to defend itself through

DOI: 10.4324/9781003132905-4

recruiting its defense mechanisms. How can the self do that? Based on the previous chapter, I will demonstrate that topographic and dynamic reorganization of the neural and psychological hierarchy of self plays a key role in constituting defense mechanisms.

Defense mechanisms II – "primacy of defense over function" vs "primacy of function over defense"

Freud himself focused especially on repression to keep painful thoughts and affects out of consciousness (see Freud 1915, as well as Bazan and Snodgras 2012; Shevrin et al. 2017; Bazan 2013; see Chapter 5 for discussion of repression in relation to consciousness). Since the early days of Freud, various other defense mechanisms, including immature and mature, have been described (see subsequently for details) (Vaillant 1992; Freud 1946; Northoff et al. 2007; Boeker et al. 2019). These include introjection and projection as well as splitting, reaction formation, identification, incorporation (and various others).

The multitude of different defense mechanisms speaks for a highly dynamic and context-dependent structure and organization, with different layers nesting within each other. This is indeed implicitly assumed when considering that later more mature defense mechanisms like reaction formation build on and are nested within the earlier rather immature defense mechanisms of splitting, projective identification, and so on. The different defense mechanisms are related to different functions. For instance, affective functions like primary and secondary emotions as well as cognitive functions like attention, memory, inhibition, and so on have been associated with different defense mechanisms in current neuropsychoanalysis (Panksepp and Biven 2012; Bazan 2013; Bazan et al. 2019; Shevrin et al. 2013; Solms 2015). The background assumption here is that the brain's functions constitute the defense mechanisms – this amounts to what I describe as "primacy of function over defense".

However, functions are determined by particular contents; the different affects are associated with different contents, and the same holds analogously for the different cognitive functions. The content-based nature of functions stands in contrast to defense mechanisms, though. Unlike functions, defense mechanisms are not determined by particular content but rather by their structure in the response to conflict. The same defense mechanisms, like splitting (or others), can be associated with different contents as well as with different affects and cognitive functions. Rather than by content, defense mechanisms must thus be defined by their structure – they reflect the structural organization of the psyche, that is, its topography and dynamic. That very same structural organization driving the defense mechanisms, in turn, strongly shapes the functions, including their content. This amounts to what I refer to as "primacy of defense over function".

The reversal in the relationship of defense and function carries major implications for how to link defense mechanisms to the brain. If defense mechanisms are based on structure rather than content and function, we need to take into view the brain's spatial topography and temporal dynamics rather than its various functions. Neuronally, defense mechanisms may then be closely related to the hierarchical balance of the three layers of self as well as to its scale-free integration of slow and fast dynamics within the power spectrum. Taken in this sense, defense mechanisms can be viewed as preservation and/or reorganization of the brain-based topography and dynamic of self. We will describe defense mechanisms in such a topographic and dynamic sense in the first part, which is complemented by dissociation as a paradigmatic example in the second part.

Part I: defense mechanisms

"Primacy of self over defense" vs "primacy of defense over self"

Defense mechanisms are closely related to the self. They are mechanisms of the self to maintain its own stability and protect itself against conflict resulting from non-self-specific events within the internal and/or external environment. Put simply, defense mechanism are the tools of the self that it uses to defend and preserve its own intrinsic structure and organization, that is, its topography and dynamic.

In that sense, defense mechanisms can be compared to the body's immune defense. The immune system recruits and constitutes antibodies to protect and defend the internal body against external invaders like antigens such as viruses and bacteria. Analogously, defense mechanisms can be conceived as the "psychological immune system" of the self on a psychological level: here traumatic events and conflicts take on the role of the antigens like viruses or bacteria in the case of the physiological immune system. Following the analogy of the immune system, we here conceive defense mechanisms in a primarily biological way: they serve to defend the self.

Different relationships of self and defense mechanisms can be conceived. One way is to conceive the self as secondary to result from the more primary defense mechanisms, or, alternatively, the defense mechanisms may be secondary to the primary self. Let us start with the first option. In current neuroscience and psychology, the self is often determined by particular bodily and/or cognitive contents resulting from the integration of the various sensory, affective, and cognitive functions (Northoff 2016b).

Since it is defined by contents based on the integration of diverse functions, the self is here conceived as a higher-order function itself – this amounts to a higher-order model of self. Applying such a higher-order model of self, one would conceive the self to be constituted by the defense mechanisms: putting and integrating all defense mechanisms together yields a self. This amounts to "primacy of defense over self".

However, the assumption of the "primacy of defense over self" conflicts with the psychodynamic role of defense mechanisms, that is, defending and protecting the self. Only if there is a self, in whatever gestalt, is there something to defend. One would then assume that the self is more basic and fundamental, which, in a second step, invokes defense mechanisms to protect itself against external events. Now the self or ego is supposed to provide the basis or fundament, which, in turn, gives rise to the defense mechanisms. This entails "primacy of self over defense".

"Primacy of self over defense" – basis model of self-specificity

Presupposing primacy of self over defense entails that the self is primary, while defense mechanisms are secondary: only if there is some kind of self can it be defended. If, in contrast. there is no self, there is nothing to defend, rendering defense mechanisms superfluous. The self must then be the most basic and fundamental function, as has been postulated in the "basis model of self-specificity" (BMSS) (Northoff 2016b; Scalabrini et al. 2020, 2022).

In a nutshell, the BMSS supposes that the self is a basic and fundamental feature that provides the basis for subsequent affective, cognitive, sensory, motor, and social function. What exactly is meant by "basis" here? Rather than providing contents specifically related to the self like self-referential contents such as one's own name or face, "basis" refers here to structure and organization, namely topography and dynamics. By constituting a particular dynamic and topography, the self structures and organizes the various contents of affective, cognitive, sensory, motor, and social functions. Constituting such a temporo-spatial basis, the self operates on a deeper and more fundamental level than the various functions while at the same time organizing and structuring them in a self-specific way, hence the name "basis model of self-specificity".

How can we support the BMSS with its assumption of such a deeper level of self on neuronal grounds? One line of support consists in the distinction of resting state and task-related activity. The self as higher-order function is typically associated with specific forms of task-related activity during self-referential stimuli (own face or name) as distinguished from non-self-referential inputs (like another person's name or face). This is the different in the case of the self as basis. In that case, the self is related to the brain's spontaneous activity, remaining independent of particular tasks or stimuli, that is, task-related activity.

Various studies of the brain's spontaneous activity suggest that its dynamic, like its power law exponent (as measured during the resting state), is directly related to the degree of self-consciousness (Chapter 1). This suggests that the self is encoded by the spontaneous activity in primarily spatiotemporal (rather than cognitive and thereby content-based) terms. Together, these studies, as described in detail in Chapter 1, support the view of the self as basis and fundamental features as explicated in the BMSS as distinguished from the traditional higher-order model of self.

We need to be careful with the seemingly clear-cut distinction of self and defense mechanisms, though. There is, for instance, no clear distinction of antibody and antigen in the physiological immune system. Analogously, there may not be clear-cut distinction of self and defense mechanisms either. Especially the early and immature defense mechanisms of internalization and externalization (see subsequently for details) like incorporation and excorporation, introjection and projection, and identification and self-objectification not only defend a pre-existing self but, at the same time, also constitute the self. This pertains to a double role of the defense mechanisms for the self including not only (i) protection and defense of the self but also (ii) constitution or construction of the topography and dynamic of the self.

Defense mechanisms – balance of internal self and external objects/environment

Defending and protecting the internal self against conflicts most often resulting from external events pits the defense mechanisms right "in-between" internal self and external objects, namely self and environment. They are neither purely internal, for example, related to the self, nor completely external, such as originating in the environment. Instead, defense mechanisms provide the connection of internal self and external environment, that is, the "self-environment connection", as I say, which, psychodynamically put, could be rephrased as "self-object relation or connection" (Spagnoli and Northoff 2021). Due to their "location" at the interface of self and environment, defense mechanisms are both intra-psychic and inter-personal at the same time – Mentzos (1992) therefore speaks of "psycho-social arrangements".

Put in a metaphorical way, defense mechanisms establish the highways between self/ego and environment/object. Due to the fact that they constitute the internal–external highways, defense mechanisms are manifest in behavior, reflecting how the self navigates within its respective environmental context. Different defense mechanisms thus go along with different forms or patterns of behavior. For instance, more mature defense mechanisms like reaction formation only induce neurotic behavior, while otherwise behavior remains relatively "normal". In contrast, the predominance of early, more immature defense mechanisms like projection and introjection induces severe changes in behavior, like psychotic or depressed behavior.

Together, defense mechanisms are neither purely internal, that is, self, nor entirely external, that is, environment. Instead, they constitute different balances of internal self and external environment, that is, self–environment connection. This can already be seen in the case of internalization and externalization that refer to different directions within the relationship of self and environment, namely from object/environment to self and from self to object/ environment. Such internal–external balance is well reflected in the following quote by Melanie Klein, who speaks of "giving in" (as corresponding to internalization) and "taking out" (as corresponding to externalization):

> the ego can then also feel that it is able to reintroject the love it has given out, as well as take in goodness from other sources, and thus be enriched by the whole process. In other words, in those cases there is a balance between giving out and taking in between introjection and projection.
>
> (1955, 312–313; see also Kernberg 1966, 364–365)

Internalization vs externalization

The most basic and therefore early and immature defense mechanisms are those related to internalization and externalization. Roughly, internalization means that something from the outside environment, that is, objects, are related to the inside of the self, while externalization describes the reverse direction, that is, from the inside of the self to the outside of the environment. This means that both establish "highways" between self and environment, albeit in different directions: internalization constitutes the "highway" from the environment/object to the self, while externalization describes the "highway" on the other side leading in the opposite direction.

Both internalization and externalization can be conceived of as umbrella terms for various defense mechanisms. Establishing the direction from object to self, internalization can play out in distinct ways like in incorporation, where an external object is integrated within and becomes part of the self with no boundaries at all anymore, as when a baby includes the mother as part of her/his own self. There is also introjection, where an external object is not integrated but closely attached and related to the self with somewhat blurry boundaries. Finally, one may also include identification, where the self transiently identifies itself with an external object while both remaining clearly separate, like a soccer fan identifying her/himself with the soccer match, but only for the latter's duration.

This is analogously so in the case of externalization, which describes the reverse direction from self to object. This includes ex-corporation, where the self is located outside the internal space of body and mind in the external environment, like when attributing ownership of one's thoughts to another person. Moreover, there is projection, where some parts of the inside of the self are located outside in the environment, like in hallucination or delusion. Finally, self-objectification is prevalent when the own self is considered and referred to only from the third-person perspective but no longer in first-person perspective.

Together, defense mechanisms refer to the internal–external relationship of self and environment. Moreover, as in the topography of self, there seem to be different layers of defense mechanisms like different layers of highways superseding each other when connecting self and environment. How these different layers of defense mechanisms are related to the self with its three-layer topography and temporal slow–fast hierarchy remains open at this point.

"Primacy of defense over function" vs "primacy of function over defense"

Defense mechanisms are manifest and expressed primarily in affect and emotion (rather than in cognition). Let us portray the example of introjection that refers to the degree to which an object of the external environment is internalized by the own self. We can see that introjection is closely related to different psychological functions. For instance, Otto Kernberg describes the affective coloring of introjection:

> The affective coloring of introjection is an essential part of it and represents the active valence of introjection, which determines

the fusion and organization of introjections of similar valences. Thus, introjection taking place under the positive valence of libidinal instinctual gratification, as in loving mother–child contact, tend to fuse and become organized in what has been called somewhat loosely, but pregnantly, the "good internal object". Introjections taking place under the negative valence of aggressive drive derivates tend to fuse with similar negative valence introjections and become organized in the "bad internal objects".

(1966, 360–361)

Yet another example of the strong affective coloring is depression or major depressive disorder (MDD), where introjection is most prominent. Excessive degrees of introjection are here manifest in an extremely strong focus on the self, that is, increased self-focus (Northoff et al. 2011; Northoff 2016a; Scalabrini et al. 2020), which, in turn, induces strong negative emotions like sadness and guilt. That further supports the major importance of affect and emotion in expressing defense mechanisms (see also Panksepp and Biven 2012). However, the close coupling of defense mechanisms and affect/emotion should not deceive one to postulate that the latter constitute the former: this would be to confuse the expression/manifestation of defense mechanisms in terms of affect/emotion with their constitution at the more basic interface of self and environment when encountering conflict.

More generally, we need to avoid slipping back into the what I described as the "primacy of function over defense". Such a view still seems to predominate in psychoanalysis, as expressed by Kernberg:

I will consider introjections as independent psychic structures, mainly growing out of primary autonomous functions (perception and memory) as they are linked with early object relationships, and although introjections will be seen as strongly influenced by oral conflicts, they will not be seen as growing out of them.

(1966, 358–359)

Current neuropsychoanalysis seems to pursue an analogous strategy, as defense mechanisms are often associated with particular affective or cognitive functions (Panksepp and Biven 2012; Solms

2015; Bazan 2013; Shevrin et al. 2013; Bazan et al. 2019). This still presupposes the "primacy of function over defense". Instead, we here suggest to consider the reverse direction, where defense mechanisms shape and are manifest in affective and cognitive function, that is, the "primacy of defense over function". How can we describe defense mechanisms, though, if not in cognitive and affective terms? This leads us to the deeper layer of the mind, namely its spatiotemporal constitution in terms of topography and dynamic. Defense mechanisms are then conceived as particular spatiotemporal constellations featuring a specific topography and dynamic – this will be illustrated by the example of dissociation in the second part of this chapter.

Brain and defense mechanisms – topography and dynamic

How can we describe defense mechanisms if not by specific sensory, affective, and/or cognitive function? For that we need to take into view the deeper level of the psyche, its topography and dynamic and how that is mediated by a more or less analogous topography and dynamic of the brain. Let us make some tentative suggestions.

The hierarchy of defense mechanisms is well established, following most often the distinction of immature and mature. Is that hierarchy related to the hierarchy of self, with its three-layer topography? Given the intimate relationship of self and defense mechanisms with the primacy of the former over the latter (see previously), one would indeed assume so. Disruptions in one layer of self may then disrupt its balance with the respective other layers of self, leading to an overall topographic reorganization – this was indicated in the case of trauma in the previous chapter.

Given the close relationship of self and defense mechanisms, we assume that the latter induce changes in the three-layer topography of the former. Moreover, the layer of self that is predominantly involved in the defense may determine the degree of maturity or immaturity of the defense mechanisms. If, for instance, the lower layer of self, the interoceptive self, is disrupted and reorganized, it may reverberate throughout both exteroceptive and mental/cognitive self – this may resemble the more immature defense mechanisms.

If, in contrast, the mental/cognitive layer of self reorganizes itself, it may be more restricted to the mental layer while leaving intero- and exteroceptive layers more or less untouched and intact – this may resemble the more mature defense mechanisms.

The same may be said about the temporal dynamic. If the slower frequencies change in their power, they may reverberate throughout the whole structure of the power spectrum, as the faster frequencies are nested within the slower ones. The whole systems' scale-freeness and long-range temporal correlations (LRTC) will change and thereby lead to reorganization of the dynamic structure of self with more immature defense mechanisms. If, in contrast, only the faster frequencies change while leaving the slower ones more or less intact, the scale-freeness and its LRTC will be essentially preserved – this may be manifest in more mature defense mechanisms.

Finally, the most fundamental change may occur when the brain's neuro-ecological, scale-free, and nested relationship with the world is disrupted. This is the case in the various layers of trauma we discussed in the second chapter. These cases share the potential mismatch between the brain's scale-freeness and the world's scale-freeness. That, in turn, disrupts the brain's neuro-ecological embedding within its respective environmental context, including its LRTC with the latter. This may, for instance, be the case in the more immature forms of internalization and externalization like projection and introjection, which are fundamentally changed in psychiatric disorders like schizophrenia and depression (Chapter 7).

Part II: dissociation

From past to present – dissociation as "out of consciousness" (Pierre Janet)

How can we illustrate such topographic and dynamic view of defense mechanisms in more detail? One key defense mechanism is dissociation that is closely linked to trauma. We have seen that trauma concerns specific event life events and contents that are threatening to the very existence of the self (Chapter 2). One way to react is to simply push those events outside consciousness – this has been described as dissociation by Pierre Janet in his original work at the end of the 19th century (see Scalabrini et al. 2020). He highlighted the abnormalities in the subjects' coordination and integration of their different psychological functions whose contents are operated in a more compartmentalized, disrupted, or dissociated way, for example, "out of consciousness":

> Unable to integrate the traumatic memories, they seem to have lost their capacity to assimilate new experiences as well. It is . . . as if their personality which definitively stopped at a certain point cannot enlarge any more by the addition of new elements.
> (Pierre Janet 1907, 532)

The central role of disrupted coordination and integration of psychological functions and their contents also resurfaces in more recent characterizations of dissociative disorders (Lanius et al. 2005; Liotti 2004). Dissociation is nowadays considered a disruption of ordinarily integrated functions in processing of mental contents as in consciousness and perception (DSM-5; American Psychiatric Association 2013) (see Scalabrini et al. 2020).

Dissociative manifestations consist in positive and negative symptomatology: (1) *positive symptoms* that are experienced as unbidden intrusions into awareness and behavior, with accompanying losses of continuity in subjective experience (i.e., fragmentation of identity, depersonalization, and derealization), and/or (ii) *negative symptoms* that are made up of the inability to access information or to control mental functions that normally are readily amenable to access or control (i.e., such as amnesia). Both positive and negative dissociative symptoms are manifested in several stress-related psychiatric dysfunctions such as post-traumatic stress disorders, dissociative disorders, and borderline personality disorders (Scalabrini et al. 2017, 2018; Lanius et al. 2012). However, the nature and mechanism of dissociation remains unclear.

Early and more recent investigators suggest additional symptoms that concern the whole personality. Specifically, Janet spoke of abnormal mental integration of the different contents, resulting in a lack of integration among two or more "systems of ideas and functions that constitute personality" (Janet 1907, 1973/1889, 1920). This is well in accordance with more recent studies that also point out abnormal integration as a structural pathology of personality (theory of structural dissociation of the personality – TSDP). One can thus speak of structural symptoms in dissociation that complement its positive and negative symptoms.

Dissociation as disrupted integration – "cracks in consciousness and brain"

Pierre Janet's characterization of dissociation as a disorder of integration strongly surfaces in our current view of dissociation. Like Janet, present descriptions clearly point out that dissociation concerns isolated contents, such as information, that are not connected, linked, or integrated with other contents. Dissociation may thus be characterized by an abnormal high degree of non-integrated information that does not become conscious. Even worse, the integration of these contents into the ongoing consciousness seems to be blocked in dissociation, with such a blockade apparently being related to the severity of the traumatic experience as marked by non-integrated contents. The parts or elements themselves are still present but remain non-integrated. Accordingly, on a psychological level, dissociation can be characterized as a disorder of integrated information, while, at the same time, non-integrated information still remains present.

Disruption in integration interferes with a coherent encoding of salient events (Scalabrini et al. 2017). That, in turn, leads to an unintegrated perception where different aspects of the event (such as sensory, affective, and cognitive) are encoded separately rather than being connected and integrated. The lack of connection and integration of sensory, affective, and cognitive aspects of events can distort one's perception including its various aspects, such as time (e.g., acting or feeling as if a traumatic event experienced in the past is still present), body (e.g., depersonalization and out of body experiences), thought (e.g., voice hearing in second-person perspective), and emotional numbing (Frewen and Lanius 2014). Positive symptoms like intrusions can then feature the perception of isolated un-integrated sensory stimuli as if the respective event is still present in time (Van der Kolk 2015; Van der Kolk et al. 1996).

In the case of negative symptoms, one may assume that the traumatic events and their contents simply "fall through the cracks of consciousness" in a rather literal way: they are no longer integrated with others, that is, non-traumatic ones, for which reason they cannot be perceived anymore, that is, they are no longer associated with consciousness at all. This is paradigmatically reflected in the loss of awareness with a continuum of different forms of des- or un-integrated contents starting from absorptions and mild gaps in awareness to more pathological manifestations such as depersonalization, derealization, and amnesia (Putnam 1995). This, as we will postulate later, may be related to "cracks in the temporo-spatial structure of the brain's spontaneous activity".

Dissociation and integration I – disrupted integration on intra-regional, inter-regional, and global levels of the brain's neural activity

In order to understand how we can link disrupted integration on the psychological level to the brain with abnormal integration on the neuronal level, we first have to briefly determine the concept of integration in a most basic and general sense (e.g., independent of either psychological or neuronal levels). Integration can be defined as the combination of different features, parts, or objects into one unified whole or unity. The different features or parts that are integrated can concern psychological functions, such as affective, sensory, cognitive, and so on, including their respective contents, while on the neuronal level, the different elements refer to the different regions' and networks' neuronal activities and how they are connected and integrated with each other.

The relationships between different brain regions are constituted by so-called "functional connectivity" (FC), which measures the degree of neuronal synchronization between different regions, shaping various neural networks in the brain's resting state (Menon 2011, for a review). Such neuronal synchronization allows integration of neuronal activity from different brain regions (and their respective psychological functions and contents) over longer stretches of time and distant regions/networks. Together, this constitutes a complex elaborated temporo-spatial structure and dynamics in the brain's spontaneous activity (Northoff 2014a and b; Northoff et al. 2020).

To better elucidate the connection between neuronal synchronization and the concept of integration, we might consider the example of the visual binding problem, that is, how different properties of an "object" might result in a unified global representation. One of the proposed solutions is based on the idea that visual objects are coded by a firing synchronization of cell assemblies. Following that hypothesis, this refers to (i) "local" integration of neuronal properties, that is, synchronization with neighboring cortical regions (deputed to the same function). This is different from (ii) "long distance" integration, that is, synchronization with distant cortical regions (deputed to different functions). Finally, there is (iii) "global" integration, that is, synchronization at the global level of the brain activity, which is necessary for the vision of the object within a more complex context of a global conscious experience. Departing from this example, one may want to distinguish between different neuronal levels of synchronization in fMRI, as on the (i) local or intra-regional level, (ii) network or inter-regional level, and (iii) global level of the whole brain. These different levels of integration will serve as a roadmap for our investigation of altered integration in dissociation.

Dissociation and integration II – disrupted integration as "common currency" of brain and psyche

How is integration on intraregional, inter-regional, and global brain levels related to integration on the psychological level? Neuronal synchronization and integration are central in constituting the spontaneous activity's temporo-spatial structure (see Scalabrini et al. 2020 for details). Even more important, based on recent data, we propose that neuronal synchronization and integration are linked on the regional, network, and global levels of the brain's neural activity; disruption of this link leads to disintegration on the psychological level, resulting in positive, negative, and structural symptoms of dissociation.

Accordingly, integration or, better, disruption of integration provides a link or bridge and thus a "common currency" (see Northoff et al. 2020) of neuronal and psychological levels in dissociation. Conceived from a historical perspective, this integration providing a "common currency" extends Janet's proposal from the psychological to the neuronal level. Integration is disrupted on both psychological and neuronal levels, for which reason neuronal changes can transform into psychological changes. What is "taken out" of the brain's neural integration and remains isolated surfaces in a more or less analogous way on the psychological level: here the respective content remains "out of consciousness" as well as unconnected and deeply isolated from other contents in the unconscious.

In sum, following and extending the original description by Pierre Janet, we here propose that dissociation is a disorder of integration on both psychological and neuronal levels. Several lines of evidence, including our own data, lend support to the assumption that integration, in dynamic and temporo-spatial terms, is disrupted on all three levels of the brain's neuronal activity, that is, regional, network, and global, in dissociative states. We assume different temporo-spatial mechanisms to be altered in dissociation. Specifically, based on the neuronal data, we assume that temporo-spatial binding of different stimuli/contents on the regional level, temporo-spatial synchronization of different functions on the network level, and temporo-spatial globalization of linking contents to level/state of consciousness on the global level are disrupted in dissociation.

Importantly, temporo-spatial integration on the three levels of the brain, that is, intra-regional, inter-regional, and global, can be linked to the different symptoms, that is, positive, negative, and structural, in dissociation. Hence, we conceive disruption in temporo-spatial integration as a "common currency" (Northoff et al. 2020) of the neuronal and psychological levels in dissociation. We therefore conclude that we can extend Pierre Janet's original concept of dissociation as disorder of integration to the brain in terms of temporo-spatial disintegration at distinct levels (intra-regional, inter-regional, global) as manifest in distinct symptoms (positive, negative, personality/global).

Conclusion

Defense mechanisms date back to the beginning of psychoanalysis and have been considerably developed since. Despite all the differences, defense mechanisms are regarded as psychological strategies to maintain and protect the self from conflicts, including both painful external events and internal memories. Current neuropsychoanalysis conceives of defense mechanisms mainly in terms of affective and cognitive functions – we therefore speak of "primacy of function over defense".

That neglects the deeper layers of our defense strategies, which are more basic and fundamental than the various functions. This deeper layer refers to the topography and dynamic of defense mechanisms, which we here explicate on both neuronal and psychological grounds. We thus characterize defense mechanisms in terms of their topography and dynamic; this allows them to connect internal self and external environment on a most basic level, prior to specific functions.

References

American Psychiatric Association (APA) (2013) Diagnostic and statistical manual of mental disorders (DSM-5®). American Psychiatric Pub, Washington, DC.

Bazan A (2013) Repression as a condition for consciousness. Neuropsychoanalysis. 15:20–23.

Bazan A, Kushwaha R, Winer ES, Snodgrass JM, Brakel LAW, Shevrin H (2019) Phonological ambiguity detection outside of consciousness and its defensive avoidance. Front Hum Neurosci. Apr 5;13:77. doi: 10.3389/fnhum.2019.00077. eCollection 2019.

Bazan A, Snodgrass M (2012) On unconscious inhibition: Instantiating repression in the brain. In: Trends in neuro-psychoanalysis: Psychology, psychoanalysis and cognitive neuroscience in dialogue (pp. 307–337), ed. A Fotopoulou, DW Pfaff, EM Conway. Oxford University Press, Oxford.

Boeker H, Hartwich P, Northoff G (Eds) (2019) Neuropsychodynamic psychiatry. Springer, Heidelberg, New York.

Freud S (1915) The unconscious (SE, Vol. 14, pp. 166–204). Hogath Press, London.

Freud S (1946) The ego and the mechanisms of defense. International University Press, New York.

Frewen PA, Lanius RA (2014) Trauma-related altered states of consciousness: Exploring the 4-D model. Journal of Trauma & Dissociation. 15(4):436–456.

Janet P (1907) The major symptoms of hysteria. Macmillan, London & New York.

Janet P (1973 [1889]) Líautomatisme psychologique: Essai de Psychologie Expérimentale sur les Formes Inférieures de L'activité Humaine. Félix Alcan, Paris; Société Pierre Janet/Payot, Paris.

Janet P (1920) The major symptoms of hysteria: Fifteen lectures given in the medical school of Harvard University. Harvard University Press, Cambridge, MA.

Kernberg O (1966) Structural derivatives of object relationships. International J of Psychoanalysis. 47:236–253.

Klein M (1955) On identification. Basic Books, New York.

Lanius RA, Brand B, Vermetten E, Frewen PA, Spiegel D (2012) The dissociative subtype of posttraumatic stress disorder: Rationale, clinical and neurobiological evidence, and implications. Depression and Anxiety. 29(8):701–708.

Lanius RA, Williamson PC, Bluhm RL, Densmore M, Boksman K, Neufeld RW, . . . Menon RS (2005) Functional connectivity of dissociative responses in posttraumatic stress disorder: A functional magnetic resonance imaging investigation. Biol Psychiatry. 57(8):873–884.

Liotti G (2004) Trauma, dissociation, and disorganized attachment: Three strands of a single braid. Psychotherapy: Theory, Research, Practice, Training. 41(4):472.

Menon V (2011) Large-scale brain networks and psychopathology: A unifying triple network model. Trends Cogn Sci. Oct;15(10):483–506. doi: 10.1016/j.tics.2011.08.003. Epub 2011 Sep 9.

Mentzos S (1992) Psychose und Konflikt. Vandenhoeck und Rupprecht, Goettingen.

Northoff G (2014a and b) Unlocking the brain. Vol. I Coding; Vol II Consciousness. Oxford University Press, Oxford, New York.

Northoff G (2016a) Spatiotemporal psychopathology I: No rest for the brain's resting state activity in depression? Spatiotemporal psychopathology of depressive symptoms. J Affect Disord. Jan 15;190:854–866. doi: 10.1016/j.jad.2015.05.007. Epub 2015 May 14. PMID: 26048657 Review.

Northoff G (2016b) Is the self a higher-order or fundamental function of the brain? The "basis model of self-specificity" and its encoding by the brain's spontaneous activity. Cogn Neurosci. Jan–Oct;7(1–4):203–222. doi: 10.1080/17588928.2015.1111868. Epub 2016 Feb 1. PMID: 26505808.

Northoff G, Bermpohl F, Schoeneich F, Boeker H (2007) How does our brain constitute defense mechanisms? First-person neuroscience and psychoanalysis. Psychother Psychosom. 76(3):141–153. doi: 10.1159/000099841

Northoff G, Wainio-Theberge S, Evers K (2020) Is temporo-spatial dynamics the "common currency" of brain and mind? In quest of "spatiotemporal neuroscience". Phys Life Rev. Jul;33:34–54. doi: 10.1016/j.plrev.2019.05.002. Epub 2019 May 23.

Northoff G, Wiebking C, Feinberg T, Panksepp J (2011) The "resting-state hypothesis" of major depressive disorder-a translational subcortical-cortical framework for a system disorder. Neurosci Biobehav Rev. Oct;35(9):1929–1945. doi: 10.1016/j.neubiorev.2010.12.007. Epub 2010 Dec 28. PMID: 21192971 Review.

Panksepp J, Biven L (2012) The archaeology of mind. Norton Publisher, New York.

Putnam FW (1995) Traumatic stress and pathological dissociation. Annals of the New York Academy of Sciences. 771(1):708–715.

Scalabrini A, Cavicchioli M, Fossati A, Maffei C (2017) The extent of dissociation in borderline personality disorder: A meta-analytic review. J Trauma Dissociation. Jul–Sep;18(4):522–543. doi: 10.1080/15299732.2016.1240738. Epub 2016 Sep 28.

Scalabrini A, Mucci C, Esposito R, Damiani S, Northoff G (2020) Dissociation as a disorder of integration: On the footsteps of Pierre Janet. Prog Neuropsychopharmacol Biol Psychiatry. Jul 13;101:109928. doi: 10.1016/j.pnpbp.2020.109928. Epub 2020 Mar 16.

Scalabrini A, Mucci C, Northoff G (2018) Is our self related to personality? A neuropsychodynamic model. Front Hum Neurosci. Oct 4;12:346. doi: 10.3389/fnhum.2018.00346. eCollection 2018.

Scalabrini A, Schimmenti A, De Amicis M, Porcelli P, Benedetti F, Mucci C, Northoff G (2022) The self and its internal thought: In search for a psychological baseline. Conscious Cogn. Jan;97:103244. doi: 10.1016/j.concog.2021.103244. Epub 2021 Nov 27.

Scalabrini A, Vai B, Poletti S, Damiani S, Mucci C, Colombo C, Zanardi R, Benedetti F, Northoff G (2020) All roads lead to the default-mode network-global source of DMN abnormalities in major depressive disorder. Neuropsychopharmacology. Nov;45(12):2058–2069. doi: 10.1038/s41386-020-0785-x. Epub 2020 Aug 2.

Shevrin H, Snodgrass M, Brakel LA, Kushwaha R, Kalaida NL, Bazan A (2013) Subliminal unconscious conflict alpha power inhibits supraliminal conscious symptom experience. Front Hum Neurosci. Sep 5;7:544. doi: 10.3389/fnhum.2013.00544. eCollection 2013.

Solms M (2015) The feeling brain. Routledge, London, New York.

Spagnoli R, Northoff G (2021) The dynamic self. Routledge Publisher, London, New York.

Steinig J, Bazan A, Happe S, Antonetti S, Shevrin H (2017) Processing of a subliminal rebus during sleep: Idiosyncratic primary versus secondary process associations upon awakening from REM- versus non-REM-sleep. Front Psychology. Nov 20;8:1955. doi: 10.3389/fpsyg.2017.01955. eCollection 2017.

Vaillant G (1992) Ego mechanisms of defense. American Psychiatric Association Press, Washington, DC.

Van der Kolk BA, Pelcovitz D, Roth S, Mandel FS (1996) Dissociation, somatization, and affect dysregulation. The American Journal of Psychiatry. 153(7):83.

Chapter 4

Cathexis and free energy

Introduction

What is cathexis? The concept of cathexis has a difficult history. Originally it was to designate what Freud described as *Besetzung* in German, which translates into "occupation" in English. However, the meaning of cathexis extends far beyond that: occupation or *besetzung* is only the result or outcome of an underlying complex process that consists and is maintained by recruiting and investing energy. Cathexis has therefore been reserved for describing the "investment of energy" (Hoffer 2005).

Note that energy and investment are here understood in a purely psychical or psychological way. The psyche is characterized by energy, that is, mental or psychic energy, which can be understood in either mechanical or dynamic terms. If understood in purely mechanical terms, cathexis invokes the image of a machine-like function entailing clear-cut separation between cause and effect as well as discontinuity with discrete points in time and space. This is probably what Freud had in mind when, in his 1895 writing "Project for a Scientific Psychology", he associated cathexis with the discharge of electrochemical energy in the brain as hydraulic machine. That entails a mechanistic understanding of cathexis in terms of cause–effect and temporal discontinuity.

However, in parallel, he also implies a more dynamic understanding of cathexis on the psychological level when he associates it with drives, libido, and motivation. These psychological or behavioral concepts no longer allow clear-cut separation between cause and

DOI: 10.4324/9781003132905-5

effect. Moreover, they presuppose some kind of temporal and spatial continuity beyond the discontinuity of discrete points in time and space: libido, drive, and motivation extend and connect different points in time and space. Together, this amounts to a more dynamic meaning of cathexis beyond both cause–effect distinction and temporo-spatial discontinuity.

Such a dynamic understanding of cathexis on the psychological level is well reflected in the following quote:

> I will add the further comment that the psychical topography that I have developed here has nothing to do with the anatomy of the brain, and actually only touches it at one point. What is unsatisfactory in this picture – and I am aware of it as clearly as anyone – is due to our complete ignorance of the *dynamic* nature of the mental processes. We tell ourselves that what distinguishes a conscious idea from a preconscious one, and the latter from an unconscious one, can only be a modification, or perhaps a different distribution, of psychical energy. We talk of cathexes and hypercathexes, but beyond this we are without any knowledge on the subject or even any starting-point for a serviceable working hypothesis. Of the phenomenon of consciousness we can at least say that it was originally attached to perception. All sensations which originate from the perception of painful, tactile, auditory or visual stimuli are what are most readily conscious. Thought-processes, and whatever may be analogous to them in the id, are in themselves unconscious and obtain access to consciousness by becoming linked to the mnemic residues of visual and auditory perceptions along the path of the function of speech.
>
> (Freud 1939, 96; italics added)

Rather than adhering to a more or less mechanical view of cathexis as it resurfaces in current neuroscientific views (see Solms 2015; Northoff 2011; Carthart-Harris and Friston 2010; Panksepp and Biven 2012), I here follow a radical dynamic view of cathexis. Specifically, I propose that the brain exhibits exactly the kind of global dynamic that constitutes its energy, that is, cathexis, which, even more importantly, the brain invests into its relationship with the environment as a basis for what psychoanalysis describes as object relation. This will be shown by the brain's global brain dynamic and topography (first part) as well as by demonstrating the temporal-dynamic underpinnings of Karl Friston's concept of "free energy" (second part). I conclude that cathexis is related to the brain's energy, namely its global dynamic and topography: these are invested into the brain's relation to its environment, thereby constituting the physiological basis for object relation on the psychological level.

Part I: cathexis and global brain dynamic

Cathexis – subcortical vs cortical sources

Drives, motivation, and libido as the psychological manifestations of cathexis have been associated mainly with subcortical regions in recent neuropsychoanalysis (Solms 2015, 2020, 2021; Panksepp and Biven 2012). This has been strongly reinforced by the close link of cathexis with primary emotions that are also "located" mainly in subcortical regions (Panksepp and Biven 2012). Does this mean that the brain's energy, that is, its cathexis, is located in mainly subcortical regions, as these observations seem to suggest? Such a view presupposes a somewhat localizationist view of the brain where different functions like energy or cathexis and others like libido, motivation, and drives are associated with a particular set of regions, areas, or networks in the brain.

However, we will see now that the brain also exhibits a global activity that spans more or less all regions and networks, including subcortical and cortical. Importantly, that very same global activity seems to be key in assigning activity to local regions and networks; that is, the global activity is represented locally in distinct degrees in different regions – this amounts to a particular topography of global brain activity. Finally, we will see that the level of such global activity is related to the degree of arousal. Together, this suggests a more global subcortical–cortical view of the brain's cathexis that carries major implications for its manifestation on the psychological level.

From global to local brain activity – global signal and its topography

The relationship between global and local activity changes is a common phenomenon in the natural world, which, among other examples of complex systems, can be observed in climate change and economy. Global warming of the earth atmosphere affects the climate in different countries and continents in different ways depending on their respective local-regional features (like ice melting in colder regions and creation of deserts in warmer regions) (Bindoff et al. 2013; Oppenheimer et al. 2015). Similarly, the global economy strongly affects economies in different countries, albeit in different ways, depending, among other factors, on the level of their development (Goldberg and Pavcnik 2007; Rodrik 2008). What holds for climate and economy may also apply to the brain as another complex system in a more or less analogous way.

Recent evidence suggests that the brain too displays "global" activity (see subsequently for defining the term "global") that modulates and is represented in different ways in its various local regions and networks. That may, in part, be related to subcortical–cortical modulation: subcortical nuclei like the serotoninergic raphe nucleus, acetylcholinergic nucleus basalis of Meynert, and dopaminergic substantia nigra modulate cortical activity in a multiregional "global" way, including the balances between different networks (Conio et al. 2020; Grandjean et al. 2019; Zerbi et al. 2019). Additionally, recent studies in animals show that multiple regions are implicated in inducing and mediating one specific behavior (Stringer et al. 2019) – this supports the potential role of the brain's more global activity in behavior.

Recent studies combining ECoG/electrophysiology and fMRI demonstrate a direct relationship of fMRI-based global brain activity as measured by the global signal (GS) with electrophysiological measures; these findings suggest that GS is not merely non-neuronal noise but also an important source of neuronal activity itself (Scholvinck et al. 2010; Wen and Liu 2016) (see subsequently for details). Furthermore, various studies show that GS is represented in different degrees in different regions: it displays a dynamic topography, that is, GS topography (Liu et al. 2018a; Liu et al. 2018b; Zhang et al. 2020).

Global dynamic – key role of slow activity with infraslow frequencies

Reviewing several studies combining GS in fMRI with electrophysiological measurements in mainly monkeys (Chang et al. 2016; Leopold et al. 2003; Liu et al. 2018a; Scholvinck et al. 2010; Scholvinck et al. 2015; Turchi et al. 2018; Wen and Liu 2016) and humans (Wen and Liu 2016), one key electrophysiological feature is that GS is related to the band limited power of different frequency ranges in different ways. For instance, infraslow frequency ranges (<0.1 Hz) show a much higher relationship, that is, correlation, with GS than faster frequencies than those in the slower (0.1–1 Hz), and faster ranges (1–100 Hz) (Leopold et al. 2003; Scholvinck et al. 2010; Scholvinck et al. 2015). These results suggest that GS is strongly driven by the long cycle durations of the very slow, that is, infraslow frequencies (<0.1 Hz) and less so by the faster frequencies.

However, there is no uniform association of GS with infraslow frequencies, as faster frequencies may contribute, too, albeit in distinct ways. In addition to the frequency range, the degree of spatial extension or distance may be an important factor. Several studies show that slower delta/theta (1–8 Hz) and faster gamma (40–80 Hz) contribute strongly to the spatial extension of neural activity beyond single regions on the cortical level and subsequently to GS (Liu et al. 2018a; Scholvinck et al. 2015; Wen and Liu 2016). In contrast, the alpha/beta range (10–30 Hz) is not related to such global extension but remains rather local as restricted to specific regions like the visual/posterior cortex and thalamus, which decreases its contributions to GS (Chang et al. 2016; Liu et al. 2018a; Scholvinck et al. 2010; Wen and Liu 2016).

Together, these data suggest that GS displays a distinct electrophysiological basis, with different frequencies making different contributions. To put it in a nutshell: the slower the frequency range, the more and stronger its contributions to the global extension of neural activity across longer cortical distances as measured by GS (Chang et al. 2016; Liu et al. 2018a; Scholvinck et al. 2010; Wen and Liu 2016). Hence, dynamic drives topography, as the degree of spatial extension of the brain's global activity is dependent upon its slow–fast relationship.

This also makes it clear that the concept of "global" in GS is to be understood in a relative rather than absolute way: unlike in earlier theories of holism that supposed involvement of the whole brain with all regions (Lashley 1950), the term "global" designates the extension of cortical activity beyond its localization in single cortical regions, with the degree of spatial extension and the number of implicated regions being somewhat flexible. This relative meaning of the term global is further supported by the transition from global to local activity as manifest in the topography of GS, as we will see further down.

Psychic energy I – global brain activity mediates the level of arousal

There are various lines of evidence linking GS fluctuation to the level of arousal. Chang et al. (2016) take monkeys' changes from eyes closed to eyes open across time as an index of behavioral arousal. They also investigate the same monkeys in fMRI, where they observe a widespread negative correlation with behavioral arousal. The fMRI arousal index is generated by correlating the widespread arousal pattern with instantaneous single volume. Both arousal indices, fMRI and behavioral, are then correlated with each other. This yields a highly significant correlation of behavioral and fMRI arousal indices: fluctuations in the behavioral arousal index are related to corresponding fluctuations in the fMRI arousal index, whose spatial pattern is further confirmed by its similarity to an instantaneous co-activation pattern that is phase-locked to the peak of GS (Liu et al. 2018a).

In order to provide an electrophysiological basis of the fMRI index of arousal, they also obtained simultaneous ECoG measuring the beta- and theta-range power index. The fMRI index of arousal correlates significantly with the beta- and theta-range power index (15–25 and 3–7 Hz, respectively), suggesting that the widespread co-activation pattern has a distinct basis in the power spectrum (Liu et al. 2018a).

What is the neuronal origin of arousal-related GS fluctuations? The empirical findings suggest that subcortical regions related to arousal may be suitable candidates for the origin of arousal-related GS fluctuations (Liu et al. 2018a; Turchi et al. 2018). Liu et al. (2018a) demonstrate that subcortical activity exhibits correlation with the cortical GS peak, albeit in a negative way, opposite to cortical regions: the troughs of subcortical activity fluctuations correlate with cortical GS peaks, which also correlate in a positive way with activity peaks in specific cortical regions. These data suggest GS modulates neuronal activity on both the cortical and subcortical levels.

The subcortical regions correlating negatively with the cortical GS peak include the thalamus (dorsomedial), basal forebrain, and midbrain (above pons, may be substantia nigra), which all show decreased signals during cortical GS peaks (Liu et al. 2018a). The strongest subcortical decrease is observed in the basal forebrain that corresponds to the nucleus basalis of Meynert (NBM), which contains acetylcholine, which is known to modulate the arousal level.

Taken together, these findings strongly support a role of GS in mediating the level of arousal as driven by subcortical regions and their apparent anti-correlation with cortical GS. That puts into doubt recent approaches in neuropsychoanalysis that solely focus on subcortical regions like the affective approach (Solms 2015; Panksepp and Biden 2012) in a larger and more comprehensive context. Rather than single subcortical brain regions, the brain's global subcortical–cortical activity is key in mediating the brain's global energy, that is, cathexis. Moreover, we can see how the brain's global energy is key in transforming neural activity into the psychological level when mediating arousal.

Psychic energy II – global brain activity is diminished in disorders of consciousness

Various studies during anesthesia in both humans (Huang et al. 2018; Huang et al. 2016; Monti et al. 2013; Schroter et al. 2012; Tanabe et al. 2020) and animals (Hamilton et al. 2017; Liang et al. 2012; Tanabe et al. 2020), as well as unresponsive wakefulness syndrome (UWS) in humans (Huang et al. 2016), suggest that the brain's GS is strongly reduced if not absent in these states. These findings further support the assumption that the level of GS is central for maintaining the level of arousal as the most basic dimension of consciousness (see Northoff and Lamme (2020) for a review of the different theories of consciousness).

This assumption is tested in a recent study by Tanabe et al. (2020). Tanabe et al. (2020) conducted fMRI in a variety of different groups, including both animal (rat) and human anesthesia with different propofol dosages (high, medium, low) in rats and different levels (wakefulness, sedation, and anesthesia) in humans. In addition, they included human subjects suffering from minimally conscious state (MCS) and UWS as well as subjects in different sleep stages (N1–3).

They measured the amplitude of GS, as well as the functional connectivity of the GS to all single voxel/regions in the brain. Both the amplitude and functional connectivity of GS exhibit major reductions in complete anesthesia in both rats and humans as well as in N3 sleep and UWS, while the intermediate stages like sedation, medium propofol dosage, N1/N2, and MCS show intermediate levels of amplitude and functional connectivity of GS, as they are higher than during the complete of unconsciousness and lower than in the fully awake state. This further suggests that the level of GS may correspond to the level of arousal as the most basic dimension of consciousness rather than to the presumably different neuronal origins or causes of the different conditions.

In sum, GS displays a distinct electrophysiological basis and mediates the fluctuations in the level of arousal by its own fluctuations on subcortical and cortical levels. Initial evidence in humans suggests that GS is key for maintaining arousal as manifest in the state or level of consciousness. Together, this suggests that GS operates in the background of the brain–behavior relationship by providing a neural predisposition (Northoff 2013; Northoff and Heiss 2015; Northoff and Lamme 2020) for the level of arousal, that is, the level or state of consciousness, as a basis for our most basic behavioral navigation within the environment.

Global signal topography – from neuronal to psychical topography

We already pointed out that the term "global" must be understood in a relative sense, on a continuum of 100% global to 100% local. This means that, in addition to its global brain activity, GS also exhibits a certain cortical distribution, that is, topography which by itself is subject change, that is, dynamic. Depending on the ongoing global fluctuations (with troughs and peaks), different networks are transiently coupled together in what is described as a co-activation pattern (CAP) (Gutierrez-Barragan et al. 2019; Zhang et al. 2020) – this amounts to GS topography (Zhang et al. 2020; Zhang and Northoff 2022). Accordingly, one can distinguish the more global background activity from its more topographic surface, as has been proposed recently in the dual layer model (DLM) of global brain activity (Zhang and Northoff 2022).

While the previously mentioned disorders of consciousness all showed decreased global brain activity, that is, GS, they were distinguished in its exact cortical distribution, that is, GS topography. For instance, the different sleep stages like N1–3 and dreams exhibit different GS topography from each other, which also distinguishes them from anesthesia. Interestingly, the dream state includes strong concentration of the global brain activity along the cortical midline axis of the default-mode network and visual network regions (Tanabe et al. 2020). Different psychiatric disorders like schizophrenia (Yang et al. 2017), major depressive disorder (Scalabrini et al. 2020), and bipolar disorder (Zhang et al. 2019) exhibit different patterns of GS topography; these are closely related to the abnormal balances of cognitive, motor, sensory, and affective functions (Zhang and Northoff 2022).

Together, there is a continuum of global and local brain activity in that the global activity (GS) is "represented" in different degrees in different regions/networks, that is, GS topography. Hence, global brain activity may be one key component that may shape the brain's topography. The brain's topography, in turn, is key in structuring and organizing mental features like consciousness (Tanabe et al. 2020) and self (Chapter 1) – neuronal topography thus translates into mental topography.

This is akin to what Freud described as "psychical topography" on the psychological level. What determines the single content's meaning is not the local content itself but its relationship to other contents and ultimately the overall global context of contents. The brain's global topography may correspond on the neuronal level of the brain to what Freud referred to as "psychical topography" on the psychological level: the brain's topography is manifest in a somewhat analogous topographical organization of mental contents on the psychical level – topography provides the "common currency" of brain and psyche.

Part II: cathexis and free energy

Cathexis and objects – investment of energy into internal and external objects

We are now ready to come back to cathexis as discussed in the psychodynamic context. As described in the introduction, cathexis refers to the investment of energy into objects. This raises two questions. How can we determine the notion of objects in the context of energy/cathexis? Can we associate the investment of psychic energy with the energy of the brain like its global dynamic and topography? Let us start with the first question.

Energy is invested into objects; however, the meaning of objects is highly ambiguous by itself. The notion of object is here understood in a rather broad meaning of the term. Objects can be associated with external inputs and contents stemming from the environment – these are "external objects", as I say. At the same time, objects can also be associated with the own self, as in Kohut, who speaks of "self-objects" (1985). Since the self is internal rather than external, self-objects must be designated as internal objects as distinguished from the external objects originating in the environment.

The concept of internal objects means that they originate internally within the person itself. Internal objects can refer to the self of the person. But they can also refer to the thoughts of that person, their internally oriented thoughts as distinguished from externally oriented thoughts (Vanhaudenhuyse et al. 2011; Hua et al. 2021). Moreover, internal objects can refer to mental time travel into past and future, something that is described as episodic simulation in psychology (Schacter et al. 2012; Northoff 2017). This makes it clear that, if understood in a broader sense beyond the own self, internal objects refer to various forms of internally oriented cognition like self, mind-wandering, and mental time travel.

What distinguishes internal objects from external objects? Rather than originating internally within the person itself, external objects have their source or origin in the external environment outside and beyond the person itself. Hence, internal and external objects differ in their source or origin relative to the person, that is, inside or outside the person. That difference in origin or source may overshadow their similarities, though: both refer to events or objects and may therefore share the investment of energy that applies to all objects regardless of their source or origin. For instance, we see in extreme states like depression that there is abnormally strong investment of energy into internal objects, that is, own self and its self-objects, at the expense of investing energy into the external objects (see Chapter 7). Hence, cathexis drives the investment of energy into objects in general regardless of their source or origin, that is, internal or external.

Finally, the investment of energy in both internal and external objects means that cathexis is not purely intra-psychic but also inter-personal crossing the boundary of inner/internal and outer/external. This is well expressed by McIntosh:

> That the character of cathexis always infuses the character of its object, especially on the unconscious level, means that it is impossible to draw any firm line between the intrapsychic and the interpersonal. The two form a single nexus. In sum, Freud's notion of cathexis as "entering into" its objects, which finds support in recent work in cognitive psychology, has the effect of undermining the centrality of the traditional Cartesian division between the "inner" and the "outer" realms of experience.
> (1993, 10)

Cathexis and free energy – cognition and mental features

Recently, Mark Solms (2020, 2021) suggests replacing the notion of cathexis by the one of free energy as understood by Friston (Solms and Friston 2018; Solms 2020, 2021). He proposes to apply the various formalism and algorithms of the free energy principle (FEP) to the psyche and its modes of operation like primary motivation, drives, libido, and so on. Psychologically, he associates that closely with affect/emotion as understood by Panksepp (Panksepp and Biven 2012). This establishes cathexis as bridge between brain and psyche, neuroscience and psychoanalysis, for which reason Solms considers the FEP a key component of a "New Scientific Psychology" (Solms 2020, 2021) (see also conclusion in this chapter).

Why does he contribute such key role of the FEP for the psyche? The free energy principle is used as a powerful formalism for modeling and understanding diverse forms of internally and externally oriented cognition, including consciousness and self. Prominent in these studies is the application of free energy to the self, as well as to different facets of self like the dynamic self, the bodily self, and the subjective self ("I" vs "me"). Together, these studies point out the key relevance of free energy and the FEP for mental features and thus for the psyche in general.

Where and how is the free energy coming from? The current neuropsychoanalytic view associates FEP with the brain itself, its inside. If, as in current neuropsychoanalysis, one equates cathexis with FEP, one would conceive cathexis as intra-psychic (and intra-neuronal). However, that will raise the question of how cathexis can be linked to object relation, which requires an inter- rather than intra-psychic relationship. This leads us back to the FEP and what exactly it signifies and aims to describe. The FEP implies that the brain is standing in continuous contact and exchange with its environmental context. That contact features their minimization of free energy within the brain's relationship to its continuously changing environmental context, which, in turn, allows the brain to reduce its own inner entropy (as too high levels of the latter would destabilize the brain). Accordingly, the FEP itself cannot be conceived as intra-neuronal nor intra-psychic but presupposes by itself the relationship of brain and environment.

"Deep temporal models" – conjoining free energy and temporo-spatial dynamic

In an attempt to constitute mental features and functions, free energy enables the brain to align to and model its ecological niche; that is, the respective environmental context. The very nature of free energy minimization – such as tuning a generative model to a hierarchical world with separation of temporal scales – necessarily means that hierarchical temporo-spatial dynamics must be recapitulated in any such aligning or adapting agent. In the language of self-organization, this is what has been described as "good regulator theorem" that describes the intimate model-like relationship between the regulator of a system and the regulated system: "every good regulator of a system must be a model of that system" (Seth 2015).

The environmental hierarchies of different events may be recapitulated and thus modelled by the brain itself within its own intrinsic hierarchical organization, that is, its temporo-spatial hierarchy. The brain's intrinsic temporo-spatial hierarchy may thus, in part, reflect a smaller scale-free version of the temporo-spatial hierarchies featuring the environment. There is no need for the living to represent a model of the environment in their head: "an agent does not *have* a model of its world – it *is* a model. In other words, the form, structure, and states of our embodied brains do not *contain* a model of the sensorium – they *are* that model" (Friston 2013). Hence, given such self-similarity between brain and environment, we may better focus on "what our head's inside of" rather than searching for "what is inside our heads" (Bruineberg and Rietveld 2014; Bruineberg et al. 2018).

How must the relationship of environment and brain be structured in order to allow such exchange and ultimately minimization of free energy? This is the moment where temporal dynamic comes in. The environmental contingencies are continuously changing, thereby reflecting the environment's "deep temporal dynamic". In order for the brain to minimize its own free energy, it must model the environment's deep temporal dynamic – this, per Friston, results in "deep temporal models" (Friston et al. 2017; Kiebel et al. 2008, 2009), entailing temporal thickness or depth (Seth 2015). These "deep temporal models" are thus crucial for the human to adjust and align their own inner temporal dynamic to the ongoing temporal dynamic of their environment. This results in a deeply temporal environment-brain/agent nexus that naturally conjoins free energy and temporo-spatial dynamics (Northoff 2019; Golesorkhi et al. 2021a, 2021b).

Deep temporal and spatial models – investment of energy into internal and external objects

Where and how can we find such deep temporal models in the brain? This leads us back to the global brain activity and specifically its dynamic and topography. We saw that the global brain dynamic is marked by very slow frequency fluctuations extending more or less throughout the whole subcortical–cortical brain (in a relative sense). This is measured by the global signal. Albeit tentatively, we assume that these very slow frequency fluctuations, through their extremely high power spectral density (which is much higher than the one of faster frequencies), provide the dynamic and thus the energy that drives the brain's neural activity to align and relate itself (in terms of free energy) with its environmental context. The brain's global dynamic may thus be key in providing energy to the brain's neural activity at its interface with the environment.

The energy provided by the very slow frequency fluctuations of the global dynamic reflects only one half of cathexis, though. While cathexis refers to energy, it refers specifically to the investment of that energy into objects. We consequently need to link the brain's global dynamic to the processing of internal and external objects. This, as we tentatively assume, may be related to the brain's global topography. We saw in the first part that the global subcortical–cortical dynamic is manifest (and "represented") in different degrees in different regions/networks – this amounts to global topography. Importantly, each of these regions or networks is implicated in the processing of particular inputs of both internal and external sources, that is, internal and external objects.

We are now ready to formulate a specific hypothesis about global brain dynamic and cathexis. We assume that the degree to which the brain's subcortical–cortical global dynamic is manifest in specific cortical regions/networks is related to the degree to which the former's energy is invested in specific objects within the environment (as processed in particular regions/networks). The more the global dynamic is present in, for instance, the default-mode network, the more energy will be investigated into its respective inputs and its associated internal objects related to internally oriented cognition (like self-reference and mental time travel). That is, for instance, the case in depression, where we can observe increases in both global DMN activity and self-referentiality (i.e., rumination), reflecting an abnormal increase in internal objects (Scalabrini et al. 2020, Chapter 7), while in mania, increased global dynamic can be observed in the motor cortex which, behaviorally, is manifest in psychomotor agitation, which psychodynamically may be associated with an increase in external objects (Zhang et al. 2019).

Together, we assume that what the concept of free energy refers to as "deep temporal models" is related to the brain's global dynamic. The brain's subcortical–cortical global dynamic provides the energy that, being manifest in different cortical regions/networks in different degrees, that is, global topography, is invested into both internal and external objects. This specifies the notion of "deep temporal models" by the global brain dynamic and, at the same time, extends it to the spatial domain, that is, "deep spatial model" referring to the brain's global topography. We assume that the brain's global dynamic and topography, through its deep spatial and temporal models provides the brain's interface with the environment, including free energy minimization. This makes it possible to invest the brain's energy into its relationship with the environment as physiological basis of what is described as cathexis on the psychological level, that is, the investment of energy into objects.

Conclusion

Cathexis is a key concept in psychoanalysis that describes the psyche's investment of energy into objects. Where and how is such energy coming from? This leads us to the brain's global dynamic and its extremely powerful very slow frequency fluctuations that extend across the whole subcortical–cortical brain. Such a global brain dynamic is manifest in different degrees in different cortical regions/ networks, amounting to global topography. Since the regions/networks process specific inputs and their respectively associated objects, we assume that the degree to which the global dynamic is manifest (or "represented") in specific regions/networks is directly related to cathexis as the investment of energy into objects.

This conjoins well with the assumption of "deep temporal and spatial models" of the free energy principle that highlights the brain's minimization of free energy with the environment. We thus provide a spatiotemporal and neuro-ecological view of the FEP that is key in linking it to cathexis as the investment of energy into object relations. What Friston describes as free energy may thus be intrinsically spatial, that is, topographic and temporal, that is, dynamic, as these provide the shared features, that is, the "common currency", of brain and environment. That "common currency", in turn, makes first and foremost possible the exchange of energy between brain and environment, that is, free energy minimization, on the physiological level as well as the investment of energy into objects, that is, cathexis, on the psychological level. Cathexis is thus primarily characterized in spatial and temporal terms that constitute its energetic and relational nature as basis for its associated affective and cognitive features (as discussed in current neuropsychoanalysis).

References

Bindoff NL, Stott PA, AchutaRao KM, Allen MR, Gillett N, Gutzler D, Hansingo K, Hegerl G, Hu Y, Jain S (2013) Detection and attribution of climate change: From global to regional. J of Climatology. 34–56.

Bruineberg J, Rietveld E (2014) Self-organization, free energy minimization, and optimal grip on a field of affordances. Front Hum Neurosci. Aug 12;8:599. doi: 10.3389/fnhum.2014.00599. eCollection 2014.

Bruineberg J, Rietveld E, Parr T, van Maanen L, Friston KJ. (2018) Free-energy minimization in joint agent-environment systems: A niche construction perspective. J Theor Biol. Oct 14;455:161–178. doi: 10.1016/j.jtbi.2018.07.002. Epub 2018 Jul 27.

Carhart-Harris RL, Friston KJ (2010) The default-mode, ego-functions and free-energy: A neurobiological account of Freudian ideas. Brain. Apr;133(Pt 4):1265–1283. doi: 10.1093/brain/awq010. Epub 2010 Feb 28.

Chang C, Leopold DA, Scholvinck ML, Mandelkow H, Picchioni D, Liu X, Ye FQ, Turchi JN, Duyn JH (2016) Tracking brain arousal fluctuations with fMRI. Proc Natl Acad Sci USA. 113:4518–4523.

Conio B, Martino M, Magioncalda P, Escelsior A, Inglese M, Amore M, Northoff G (2020) Opposite effects of dopamine and serotonin on resting-state networks: Review and implications for psychiatric disorders. Mol Psychiatry. Jan;25(1):82–93. doi: 10.1038/s41380-019-0406-4. Epub 2019 Apr 5.

Freud S (1895) Project for a scientific psychology. Hogarth Press, London.

Freud S (1939) An outline of psychoanalysis. Hogarth Press, London.

Friston KJ (2013) Life as we know it. R Soc Interface. Jul 3;10(86):20130475. doi: 10.1098/rsif.2013.0475. Print 2013 Sep 6.

Friston KJ, Rosch R, Parr T, Price C, Bowman H (2017) Deep temporal models and active inference. Neurosci Biobehav Rev. Jun;77:388–402. doi: 10.1016/j.neubiorev.2017.04.009. Epub 2017 Apr 14.

Goldberg PK, Pavcnik N (2007) Distributional effects of globalization in developing countries. Journal of economic Literature. 45:39–82.

Golesorkhi M, Gomez-Pilar J, Tumati S, Fraser M, Northoff G (2021a) Temporal hierarchy of intrinsic neural timescales converges with spatial core-periphery organization. Commun Biol. Mar 4;4(1):277. doi: 10.1038/s42003-021-01785-z

Golesorkhi M, Gomez-Pilar J, Zilio F, Berberian N, Wolff A, Yagoub MCE, Northoff G (2021b) The brain and its time: Intrinsic neural timescales are key for input processing. Commun Biol. Aug 16;4(1):970. doi: 10.1038/s42003-021-02483-6

Grandjean J, Corcoba A, Kahn MC, Upton AL, Deneris ES, Seifritz E, Helmchen F, Mann EO, Rudin M, Saab BJ (2019) A brain-wide functional map of the serotonergic responses to acute stress and fluoxetine. Nat Commun. 10:350.

Gutierrez-Barragan D, Basson MA, Panzeri S, Gozzi A (2019) Infraslow state fluctuations govern spontaneous fMRI network dynamics. Curr Biol. 29:2295–2306, e2295.

Hamilton C, Ma Y, Zhang N (2017) Global reduction of information exchange during anesthetic-induced unconsciousness. Brain Struct Funct. 222:3205–3216.

Hoffer PT (2005) Reflections on cathexis. The Psychoanalytic Quarterly. 74:1127–1135.

Hua J, Zhang Y, Wolff A, Northoff G (2021) Thought dynamics is mediated by alpha and theta peak frequency. Nature Communication Biology, in press.

Huang Z, Liu X, Mashour GA, Hudetz AG (2018) Timescales of intrinsic BOLD signal dynamics and functional connectivity in pharmacologic and neuropathologic states of unconsciousness. J Neurosci. 38:2304–2317.

Huang Z, Zhang J, Wu J, Qin P, Wu X, Wang Z, Dai R, Li Y, Liang W, Mao Y, Yang Z, Zhang J, Wolff A, Northoff G (2016) Decoupled temporal variability and signal synchronization of spontaneous brain activity in loss of consciousness: An fMRI study in anesthesia. Neuroimage. 124:693–703.

Kiebel SJ, Daunizeau J, Friston KJ (2008) A hierarchy of time-scales and the brain. PLoS Comput Biol. Nov;4(11):e1000209. doi: 10.1371/journal.pcbi.1000209. Epub 2008 Nov 14.

Kiebel SJ, Daunizeau J, Friston KJ (2009) Perception and hierarchical dynamics. Front Neuroinform. Jul 20;3:20. doi: 10.3389/neuro.11.020.2009. eCollection 2009.

Kohut H (1985) How does analysis cure? Chicago University Press, Chicago.

Lashley KS (1950) In search of the engram. Symposia of the Society for Experimental Biology. 4:454–482.

Leopold DA, Murayama Y, Logothetis NK (2003) Very slow activity fluctuations in monkey visual cortex: Implications for functional brain imaging. Cereb Cortex. 13:422–433.

Liang Z, King J, Zhang N (2012) Intrinsic organization of the anesthetized brain. J Neurosci. 32:10183–10191.

Liu X, de Zwart JA, Scholvinck ML, Chang C, Ye FQ, Leopold DA, Duyn JH (2018a) Subcortical evidence for a contribution of arousal to fMRI studies of brain activity. Nat Commun. 9:395.

Liu X, Zhang N, Chang C, Duyn JH (2018b) Co-activation patterns in resting-state fMRI signals. Neuroimage. 180:485–494.

McIntosh D (1993) Cathexis and their objects in the thought of Sigmund Freud. J of the American Psychoanalytic Association. 41(3):679–709.

Monti MM, Lutkenhoff ES, Rubinov M, Boveroux P, Vanhaudenhuyse A, Gosseries O, Bruno MA, Noirhomme Q, Boly M, Laureys S (2013) Dynamic change of global and local information processing in propofol-induced loss and recovery of consciousness. PLoS Comput Biol. 9:e1003271.

Northoff G (2011) Neuropsychoanalysis in practice. Oxford University Press, Oxford, New York.

Northoff G (2013) What the brain's intrinsic activity can tell us about consciousness? A tri-dimensional view. Neurosci Biobehav Rev. May;37(4):726–738. doi: 10.1016/j.neubiorev.2012.12.004. Epub 2012 Dec 17.

Northoff G (2017) Personal identity and cortical midline structures. Psychological Inquiry. 34–45.

Northoff G (2019) Lessons from astronomy and biology for the mind-Copernican revolution in Neuroscience. Front Hum Neuroscience. Sep 19;13:319. doi: 10.3389/fnhum.2019.00319. eCollection 2019.

Northoff G, Heiss W-D (2015) Why is the distinction between neural predispositions, prerequisites, and correlates of the level of consciousness clinically relevant? Functional brain imaging in coma and vegetative state. Stroke. 46:1147–1151.

Northoff G, Lamme V (2020) Neural signs and mechanisms of consciousness: Is there a potential convergence of theories of consciousness in sight? Neuroscience & Biobehavioral Reviews. In press.

Oppenheimer M, Campos M, Warren R, Birkmann J, Luber G, O'Neill B, Takahashi K, Brklacich M, Semenov S, Licker R (2015) Emergent risks and key vulnerabilities (pp. 1039–1100) (Climate Change 2014 Impacts, Adaptation and Vulnerability: Part A: Global and Sectoral Aspects). Cambridge University Press, Cambridge.

Panksepp J, Biven L (2012) The archaeology of mind. Norton Publisher, New York.

Rodrik D (2008) One economics, many recipes: Globalization, institutions, and economic growth. Princeton University Press, Princeton, NJ.

Scalabrini A, Vai B, Poletti S, Damiani S, Mucci C, Colombo C, Zanardi R, Benedetti F, Northoff G (2020) All roads lead to the default-mode network-global source of DMN abnormalities in major depressive disorder. Neuropsychopharmacology. 45:2058–2069.

Schacter DL, Addis DR, Hassabis D, Martin VC, Spreng RN, Szpunar KK (2012) The future of memory: Remembering, imagining, and the brain. Neuron. Nov 21;76(4):677–694. doi: 10.1016/j.neuron.2012.11.001

Scholvinck ML, Maier A, Ye FQ, Duyn JH, Leopold DA (2010) Neural basis of global resting-state fMRI activity. Proc Natl Acad Sci USA. 107:10238–10243.

Scholvinck ML, Saleem AB, Benucci A, Harris KD, Carandini M (2015) Cortical state determines global variability and correlations in visual cortex. J Neurosci. 35:170–178.

Schroter MS, Spoormaker VI, Schorer A, Wohlschlager A, Czisch M, Kochs EF, Zimmer C, Hemmer B, Schneider G, Jordan D, Ilg R (2012) Spatiotemporal reconfiguration of large-scale brain functional networks during propofol-induced loss of consciousness. J Neurosci. 32:12832–12840.

Seth AK (2015) Presence, objecthood, and the phenomenology of predictive perception. Cogn Neurosci. 6(2–3):111–117. doi: 10.1080/17588928.2015.1026888. Epub 2015 Apr 7.

Solms M (2015) The feeling brain. Routledge, London, New York.

Solms M (2020) Project for a (new) psychology. Neuropsychoanalysis. 23–45.

Solms M (2021) The hidden spring: A journey to the source of consciousness. Norton Publisher, New York.

Solms M, Friston K (2018) Why and how consciousness arises? Some considerations from physics and biology. Journal of Consciousness Studies. 25(5–6).

Stringer C, Pachitariu M, Steinmetz N, Reddy CB, Carandini M, Harris KD (2019) Spontaneous behaviors drive multidimensional, brainwide activity. Science. 364:255.

Tanabe S, Huang Z, Zhang J, Chen Y, Fogel S, Doyon J, Wu J, Xu J, Zhang J, Qin P, Wu X, Mao Y, Mashour GA, Hudetz AG, Northoff G (2020) Altered global brain signal during physiologic, pharmacologic, and pathologic states of unconsciousness in humans and rats. Anesthesiology. 132:1392–1406.

Turchi J, Chang C, Ye FQ, Russ BE, Yu DK, Cortes CR, Monosov IE, Duyn JH, Leopold DA (2018) The basal forebrain regulates global resting-state fMRI fluctuations. Neuron. 97:940–952 e944.

Vanhaudenhuyse A, Demertzi A, Schabus M, Noirhomme Q, Bredart S, Boly M, Phillips C, Soddu A, Luxen A, Moonen G, Laureys SJ (2011) Two distinct neuronal networks mediate the awareness of environment and of self. Cogn Neurosci. Mar;23(3):570–8. doi: 10.1162/jocn.2010.21488. Epub 2010 Jun 1.

Wen H, Liu Z (2016) Broadband electrophysiological dynamics contribute to global resting-state fMRI signal. J Neurosci. 36:6030–6040.

Yang GJ, Murray JD, Glasser M, Pearlson GD, Krystal JH, Schleifer C, Repovs G, Anticevic A (2017) Altered global signal topography in schizophrenia. Cereb Cortex. 27:5156–5169.

Zerbi V, Floriou-Servou A, Markicevic M, Vermeiren Y, Sturman O, Privitera M, von Ziegler L, Ferrari KD, Weber B, De Deyn PP, Wenderoth N, Bohacek J (2019) Rapid reconfiguration of the functional connectome after chemogenetic locus coeruleus activation. Neuron. 103:702–718 e705.

Zhang J, Huang Z, Tumati S, Northoff G (2020) Rest-task modulation of fMRI-derived global signal topography is mediated by transient coactivation patterns. PLoS Biol. 18:e3000733.

Zhang J, Magioncalda P, Huang Z, Tan Z, Hu X, Hu Z, Conio B, Amore M, Inglese M, Martino M, Northoff G (2019) Altered global signal topography and its different regional localization in motor cortex and hippocampus in mania and depression. Schizophr Bull. 45:902–910.

Zhang J, Northoff G (2022) Beyond noise to function: reframing the global signal and its topography in fMRI. Nature Communications Biology. In press.

Chapter 5

Unconscious and conscious

Introduction

Freud introduced the unconscious into psychology. While others like Arthur Schopenhauer and Friedrich Nietzsche had already thematized the unconsciousness in philosophy, Freud was the first to investigate it in a systematic and empirical (taken in a broad definition) way. For him the unconscious consists in innate, inherently sexual, and aggressive blind drives – we have no control over these drives. They are instinctual, non-rational, and strongly affective–emotional – psychoanalysis speaks therefore of primary process – this amounts to what Freud describes as "dynamic or repressed unconscious".

More recently these primary processes have been associated with mainly subcortical regions and their various subcortical primary emotion systems like rage, seeking, fear, panic, care, play, and lust (Panksepp 1998; Solms 2015; Panksepp and Biven 2012). Mark Solms therefore associates these subcortical emotional systems with the dynamic unconscious and its Id (Solms 2015). The primary emotions remain largely unconscious, and we have barely access to them; they are evolutionarily imprinted, so we as humans share them with our ancestors, the non-human species (Panksepp 1998).

Freud's concept of the dynamic unconscious has also been associated with the notion of the unconscious in psychology and cognitive neuroscience. Here, the unconscious has been associated with various functions like cognition, affect, behavior, memory, and so on – concepts

DOI: 10.4324/9781003132905-6

like "cognitive unconscious" (Kihlstroem 1987), "emotional unconscious" (Kihlstroem et al. 1992), "behavioral unconscious", "cognitive unconscious" (Uleman 2005), and "procedural unconscious"
Schuessler 2002) (as well as various others). In this more cognitive
context, the unconscious is associated with a particular function and its
respective content, a cognitive content in the cognitive unconscious,
an affective content in the emotional or affective unconscious, a motor
content in the procedural unconscious, and so on.

Given the prominence of contents in this more cognitive form
of unconscious as it prevails in current psychology and neuroscience, I speak of a "content-based unconscious" that signifies the
unconscious in traditional psychology. The only difference of these
content-based forms of the unconscious to the conscious is that
these contents are not yet actually conscious but may occur and
be possible at any time. What is called unconscious in current psychology and neuroscience, that is, content-based unconscious, may
therefore resemble more what Freud and psychodynamics refer
to as preconscious, as both include contents that may or may not
become conscious.

The fact that these more recent cognitive notions of the unconscious are content based and entail the possibility of contents
becoming conscious distinguishes them from Freud's concept of
the dynamic unconscious. The dynamic unconscious is neither
focused on specific content nor necessarily includes their possibility of becoming conscious. Instead, the Freudian concept of
dynamic unconscious is, as in its name, focused on the dynamic,
namely psychodynamic, that may or may not go along with specific contents.

As it extends beyond contents to dynamic, the dynamic unconscious covers a much broader and richer range than the current
content-based unconscious. In order to relate the dynamic unconscious to the brain, we need to go beyond the neural correlates of
conscious vs unconscious contents. We need to extend our view
to a deeper layer of the brain's neural activity, its topography and
dynamic. This is the main focus in this chapter: how the Freudian concept of the dynamic unconscious in terms of topography
and dynamic relates to a more or less analogous topography and
dynamic of the brain's neural activity.

Part I: preconscious and repression

Early vs late stimulus-induced activity – phenomenal and access consciousness

Within the context of neuroscience, consciousness is typically associated with specific contents. What is described as "neural correlates of consciousness" (NCC) (Koch 2004) indexes the neural features underlying the phenomenal experience of contents, the "what it is like" as the qualitative experience ("redness of red"). Such phenomenal consciousness is distinguished from becoming aware of the phenomenal experience as such – this is described as reflective or access consciousness (Block 2005; Northoff and Lamme 2020).

What are neural correlates of phenomenal and access consciousness? These are related to stimulus-induced or task-related activity including its early and late components. The bulk of the neuroscientific theories of consciousness like integrated information theory (IIT) (Tononi et al. 2016), global neuronal workspace theory (GNWT) (Mashour et al. 2020), recurrent processing theory (RPT) (Lamme 2018), and higher-order theory (HOT) (Lau and Rosenthal 2011), have focused on stimulus-induced or task-related activity.

They focus on various measures and particular regions. The IIT postulates that early changes like N100 and complexity (as measured by Lempel Zev complexity) in posterior cortical regions are key to contents becoming conscious in the sense of phenomenal consciousness, while others like HOT and GNWT postulate that later signs like P300 in prefrontal cortex are necessary for conscious contents – this has been related to reflective or access consciousness (Northoff and Lamme 2020). Without going into detail about these various measures and theories (see Northoff and Lamme 2020 for a recent detailed overview), we can see that the distinction of early (0–150 ms) and late (300–600 ms) stimulus-induced or task-related activity is associated with distinct forms of consciousness, that is, phenomenal and reflective/access consciousness.

Prestimulus activity shapes the contents of consciousness

The current neuroscientific discussion on consciousness focuses largely on stimulus-induced activity, including its early vs late components, the neural correlates of consciousness. This is well reflected in the prominence of GNWT, IIT, RPT, and HOT in the current discussion (Northoff and Lamme 2020). However, recent data show that stimulus-induced activity by itself cannot be exclusively related to consciousness. The activity prior to the stimulus, the prestimulus activity, has also been shown to play a key role in contents becoming conscious or, alternatively, remaining unconscious.

Various studies describe the impact of prestimulus activity levels on the contents and the level or state, that is, arousal of consciousness in both fMRI, EEG/MEG or single unit activity. Concerning the contents, fMRI studies showed that if the level of prestimulus activity in the fusiform face area (FFA) is high, subjects will perceive the stimulus as a face, whereas low prestimulus activity in FFA will bias subjects towards perceiving the same stimulus as a vase (Hesselmann et al. 2008; Sadaghiani et al. 2010).

The prestimulus power and phase synchrony of alpha oscillations (8–13 Hz) in the EEG strongly impacts whether one perceives a visual stimulus (Benwell et al. 2017; Dijk et al. 2008; Romei et al. 2010; Wolff et al. 2019). Other frequencies in the prestimulus period like slow cortical potentials (0.1 to 1 Hz) and delta, theta, and beta power, but also prestimulus functional connectivity, impact subsequent stimulus-related activity and its association with consciousness (Baria et al. 2017; Benwell et al. 2017; Podvalny et al. 2019; Sadaghiani et al. 2015, 2010). Finally, a recent MEG study demonstrates that prestimulus activity not only mediates specific contents of consciousness (as prestimulus activity levels predicted the subsequent contents) but also a more general process related to arousal (as indexed by pupil size) (Podvalny et al. 2019).

Prestimulus activity and preconscious

Together, these findings suggest that we need to broaden the concept of neural correlates of consciousness beyond the stimulus-induced activity itself. This has been described in neuroscience by the "neural prerequisites of consciousness" (NCC pre) (Aru et al. 2012; de Graaf et al. 2012; Northoff and Heiss 2015), namely those neural features that enable consciousness but are not by themselves sufficient for it, while psychologically, we suppose that the prestimulus activity dynamics is closely related to what Freud described as "preconscious".

The preconscious includes those contents that can become conscious while not yet being actually conscious. The recent data show that prestimulus activity and its dynamic are key in mediating the transition from unconscious to conscious contents: if the prestimulus dynamic is in the "right" configuration and encounters the "right" external input, the respective content can become conscious. If, in contrast, the prestimulus activity shows the "wrong" dynamic configuration and/or encounters the "wrong" external input, the respective content will remain within the preconscious (or remain unconscious in the sense of content-based unconscious).

How can we further characterize the contents of such a prestimulus-based preconscious? These contents that are not yet actually conscious but can in principle become conscious – they reflect what is described as "cognitive unconscious" (Kihlstroem 1987), "emotional unconscious" (Kihlstroem et al. 1992), "behavioral unconscious" (Uleman 2005), and "procedural unconscious" Schuessler 2002). These are specific contents like memories of a particular event, specific emotions, or movement pattern during dancing that are not consciously experienced but remain unconscious. Importantly, the very same contents can, at any point in time, become conscious given the "right" circumstances: psychologically, this may refer to certain life events triggering the recall of those events in memory, while neuronally we suppose that prestimulus activity levels may play a key role here.

The impact of prestimulus activity on the contents of consciousness can be compared to the situation of a surfer riding on the ocean's waves. The ocean's waves can be characterized by power, high or low, speed/frequency, that is, slow or fast, and their phase angles, that is, sharp or smooth. The surfer staying afloat (conscious, in this metaphor) depends both on the activity of the surfer (stimulus-related activity), as on the waves of the ocean (prestimulus or ongoing activity). Specifically, the surfer (= stimulus-related activity) needs to adapt and integrate her/himself to the power, the speed/frequency, and the phase angle of the waves. Only if the two interact in a meaningful way does the surfer become "part of the waves" and stay erect (this showing consciousness).

In the same way, an external stimulus has to interact with ongoing activity such that the two get integrated into the current stream of consciousness. The external stimulus needs to be integrated within the power, the frequency/speed, and the phase of the ongoing spontaneous activity as measured in the prestimulus period. If the external stimulus is not integrated at all, it will not become conscious. This may occur, for instance, when a specific external stimulus "arrives" at the "wrong" point in time, like low power, too slow speed, and low excitable phase angle (like the peak rather than the trough; Huang et al. 2017) – the external stimulus may be processed but remain unconscious ("reception without perception"; Hudetz et al. 2015).

Repression and prestimulus dynamic – blocking access to the conscious

One of the key features of Freud's and others' psychodynamic view of consciousness is repression. There is an active repression mechanism. Freud assumed that this active repression mechanism is exerted by the conscious itself as it suppresses the conscious emergence of those contents of the Id threatening the ego. What exactly is repressed or inhibited? Following Freud, both action and language of the represented material that is its contents are repressed: "A representation which is not put into words, or a psychical act which is not hypercathected, remains thereafter in the unconscious" (Freud 1915, 186).

Psychologically, repression as feature of the dynamic unconscious can be tested by subliminal priming. Subliminal priming and processing allow probing for semantically meaningful association between contents that remain completely unconscious. This has been demonstrated for memory, language, motor action/control, and emotion and affect. The contents of these various function can all be suppressed or inhibited such that they cannot be put into action, words, or emotion by which they can enter the conscious. Instead, being blocked from moving to the conscious, they remain unconscious. That becomes especially strong in neurosis and its various symptoms that can be understood as "return of the repressed", which now comes to the forefront in an indirect way, that is, through abnormal affective and cognitive function.

This line has been followed and extended to neuroscience more recently by Bazan (2012, 2017) and Shevrin (Shevrin et al. 2013). They suppose that, neuronally, the alpha power is associated with repression. When, for instance, shifting from prestimulus and/or rest states to task states, the degree of alpha power decreases. That has been shown for subliminal priming and unconscious material (Shevrin et al. 2013) – decrease or suppression of alpha power may therefore be key in repressing conflictual experience such that they cannot enter the conscious. Accordingly, alpha power being key in mediating the transition from rest or prestimulus to task states may modulate the transition from the unconscious contents of the preconscious to the conscious contents of phenomenal (and ultimately access or reflective) consciousness (Bazan 2012, 2017; Shevrin et al. 2013).

These data on alpha and repression are well in accordance with the observation that prestimulus alpha levels do indeed strongly impact whether a subsequent content becomes conscious or not (Benswell et al. 2017). Hence, alpha may indeed serve a strong neural candidate that "gates" the transition from the preconscious to the conscious. If the alpha gate "does not open", the respective content remains preconscious and does not become conscious – it is thus "repressed". If, in contrast, the alpha gate is opened by lowering alpha power, the preconscious content can become conscious and is no longer "repressed".

Accordingly, what psychodynamically is described as repression may, tentatively hypothesized, correspond neuronally to the level or degree of prestimulus alpha power: how the latter is modulated, that is, decreased by the actual content of the preconscious may "decide" whether the "alpha gate" "releases" the content from its repression by "opening" the gate for the content to become conscious.

Part II: dynamic unconscious and nestedness

Temporal nestedness of stimulus-related activity within prestimulus and spontaneous activity

Prestimulus activity is just a short interval prior to the onset of the stimulus. As such, it reflects the ongoing dynamic of the brain's spontaneous activity as it can be measured in what is described as a "resting state", that is, the absence of any specific external input or stimuli. Various studies demonstrate that the resting state and thus spontaneous activity is by itself related to the level or state of consciousness.

Studies in altered states of consciousness like sleep, anesthesia or unresponsive wakefulness state (UWRS), or psychedelics show that changes in the level or state of consciousness go along with dynamic changes in the brain's spontaneous activity. For instance, the power of the slower frequencies becomes abnormally strong with weaker faster frequencies when one losses consciousness (Northoff and Lamme 2020 for overviews), while the opposite, with more power in the faster frequencies, can be observed when consciousness is enhanced, as during psychedelics (Northoff et al. 2020a, 2020b).

This can be measured by the power spectrum and especially its shape as it is operationalized by the power law exponent. Roughly, the PLE describes the shape or slope of the curve of the power spectrum with a steep decline from the strong power of slower frequencies to the weaker power of faster frequencies. This means that the weaker faster frequencies (with their shorter cycle durations) are nested and contained within the stronger slower frequencies (and their longer cycle durations). Changes in the slope of the power spectrum with altered balances towards either slower or faster frequencies thus entail shift in the slow–fast temporal dynamic including their degree of temporal nestedness.

The temporal nestedness of the power spectrum is also changed during the transition from resting state to stimulus-related activity. Stimulus-related activity induces a shift in the power spectrum towards enhancing the power of faster frequencies as measured by a decrease in the PLE (the curve of slow–fast frequencies is less steep). One can consequently say that stimulus-related activity is nested temporally within prestimulus activity which, in turn, is nested within the brain's resting state or spontaneous activity. Moreover, the data on altered states of consciousness (see previously and Northoff and Lamme 2020) strongly suggest that such temporal nestedness of stimulus-related activity within spontaneous activity is key for consciousness.

Neural correlates of consciousness and neural predispositions of consciousness

The data suggest that stimulus-related, prestimulus, and resting state activity take on different roles for consciousness. Measures of stimulus-related activity like P300 and Lempel Zev complexity (LZC) (and others; Northoff and Lamme 2020) are presumed to be sufficient neural correlates of either the phenomenal aspects of consciousness (NCC proper; Koch et al. 2016) or its cognitive aspects (by some called the consequences of consciousness: NCCcon; Aru et al. 2012). This distinguishes them from measures of prestimulus activity like prestimulus activity amplitude, synchrony, variability, or power spectrum that are supposed to enable consciousness (neural prerequisites of consciousness: preNCC; Aru et al. 2012, which used NCCpre as original transcription).

NCC and preNCC leave open more or less the role of the spontaneous activity as measured in resting state. Various studies in both healthy and neurologic/psychiatric subjects demonstrate involvement of spontaneous activity in consciousness (see previously). Its exact role remains unclear, though. Spontaneous activity by itself, that is, independent of specific stimuli or tasks as processed in stimulus-related or task-related activity, is not sufficient for the contents of consciousness. Becoming conscious of specific contents requires additional stimulus-related activity or, at least, neuronal changes in the resting state analogous to the former, amounting to "virtual" stimulus-related activity (Zhang et al. 2019, 2020).

Together, these and other findings (see previously) led to the assumption that spontaneous activity provides the necessary but not sufficient neural conditions of consciousness. Spontaneous activity provides the neural capacity or neural predisposition of consciousness

(NPC) (Northoff 2018; Northoff and Huang 2017; Northoff and Heiss 2015). Such a neural predisposition or capacity makes consciousness possible while not realizing its actual manifestation: in the absence of such a neural predisposition, consciousness will become altogether impossible, while its presence does not automatically guarantee the manifestation of actual consciousness (as additional neuronal mechanisms, that is, NCC, are required for that).

Dynamic unconscious – dynamic and topography

Spontaneous activity itself is not sufficient for consciousness while, at the same time, being necessary for it as neural predisposition. This suggests that spontaneous activity plays a key role in the unconscious, specifically, the dynamic unconscious. Roughly, giving a loose definition, the dynamic unconscious refers to the dynamic of mental contents and particular affective-cognitive constellations: these are related to the individual person or self but cannot be accessed as such by the person in their consciousness. Moreover, the mental contents and their affective constellations can change over time depending on the persons' life events and their perception of them. In other terms, one can speak of mental dynamic that as such remains largely unconscious entailing the "dynamic unconscious".

How can we support our assumption that the dynamic unconscious, as determined in psychoanalysis, is related to the neuronal dynamic of the brain's spontaneous activity? Presupposing shared features of neural and unconscious activity, that is, "common currency" (Northoff et al. 2020a, 2020b), we assume they share their dynamic: the changes of unconscious contents and their affective-cognitive constellations may be related to (and thus shared by) a more or less corresponding temporal dynamic in neural activity. Let us provide a more concrete example.

We saw that the brain's neural activity in characterized by a scale-free balance in the power of slow and fast frequencies, that is, the power law exponent. One would now assume that an analogous balance of slow and fast frequencies structures the unconscious contents, including their duration and changes. If, for instance, the brain's slow frequencies are very powerful, one would expect more longer durations in the unconscious contents with less change in more or less corresponding frequency ranges, while predominance of the faster frequencies in the brain's power spectrum should be manifest in unconscious contents of shorter duration and increased change (see Vanhaudenhuyse et al. 2011; Hua et al. 2021 for first support). This went topographically with different balances in the relationship of default-mode network and visual network (Vanhaudenhuyse et al. 2011).

In sum, the dynamic unconscious may be based on the brain's temporal dynamic and its spatial topography. Both may feature nestedness in temporal terms like slow–fast balance in the power spectrum as well as by nestedness in spatial terms like small-world organization with core-periphery organization in topography (Northoff and Huang 2017; Golesorkhi et al. 2021a, 2021b). Rather than by specific contents as consciousness, the dynamic unconscious may then primarily be determined more by its topography and dynamic that, as we assume, are shared by brain and unconscious, that is, "common currency".

Topography and dynamic – nestedness on neuronal and psychological levels

We saw nestedness throughout this chapter. Different forms of neural activity like early and late stimulus-induced activity, prestimulus activity, and resting state activity are contained and nested within each other. They can be distinguished according to the spatiotemporal scales on which they operate: resting state activity includes the largest space-time scale, whereas late stimulus-induced activity operates on a much smaller scale.

Nestedness can also be seen in the brain's spatial topography. We have seen in the previous chapter that global brain activity can differentiate itself in distinct regions, with the latter's local activity thus nesting within the former's more global activity. This can also be seen in the small world organization of the brain and its core-periphery structure. Such nestedness on the spatial-topographic side is complemented by nestedness on the temporal side: the high power of slower frequencies nests and contains the lower power of faster frequencies. Hence, one can speak of temporo-spatial nestedness.

Just like different Russian dolls contain different scales, the different layers of the brain's spatial topography and temporal dynamic are nested within each other according to their temporo-spatial scales.

Based on the empirical evidence presented previously, I now propose that such temporo-spatial nestedness of the various layers of the brain's neural activity is associated with corresponding layers of unconscious/consciousness on the psychological side. I speak of a nested hierarchy with different layers. The bottommost layer consists in the deep unconscious, followed by the dynamic unconsciousness, which, in turn, nests and contains the preconscious and the conscious.

It was one of the major insights of Freud to have recognized this more extended framework of the unconscious–conscious on the psychological level. This, albeit tentatively, can now be extended to the neuronal level of the brain and its temporo-spatial nestedness of both its topography and dynamic. Unconscious–conscious are consequently primarily spatial-topographic and temporal-dynamic features, as postulated in the temporo-spatial theory of consciousness (TTC) (Northoff and Huang 2017; Northoff and Lamme 2020; Northoff and Zilio 2021). Temporo-spatial nestedness thus provides the link if not a shared feature of brain and consciousness/unconsciousness.

Conclusion

Consciousness and unconscious are not homogenous entities but may instead be conceived as highly heterogenous and multifaceted processes, with different layers of neuronal activity nesting within each other (Northoff and Huang 2017; Northoff and Lamme 2020; Northoff and Zilio 2021). The concept of layers is used throughout this chapter to indicate nestedness: in the same way different Russian dolls nest within each other, that is, the smaller one is nested or contained within the next larger one, consciousness and the brain's neural activity are supposed to be characterized by different layers that contain and nest within each other.

Nestedness in this sense applies to both phenomenal and neuronal levels, that is, consciousness/unconsciousness and brain. That carries the consequence that the nested organization of the brain's neural activity may be related to and ultimately surface in a more or less analogous nested organization of conscious and unconscious as signified by different temporal and spatial scales. Temporo-spatial nestedness may consequently provide a "common currency" of brain and consciousness, that is, neuronal and phenomenal levels (Northoff et al. 2020a, 2020b), as postulated in the temporo-spatial theory of consciousness (Northoff and Huang 2017; Northoff and Zilio 2021).

In conclusion, we suppose that the "common currency" approach provides the key to address the "hard problem", that is, the question of why and how there is consciousness as distinct from the physical world and the brain (Chalmers 1996; Solms 2019; Northoff 2018). Because the brain exhibits a particular dynamic and topography, it predisposes and can actually manifest consciousness. It was the genius of Freud who foresaw such dynamic and topographic determination of conscious–unconscious on the level of the psychic that now can be extended to the brain, that is, its topography and dynamic. Topography and dynamic of neural activity as the brain's inside or "deep interior" (as the philosopher Thomas Nagel says; 1998) make possible and realize the different layers of unconscious and conscious as so well described by Freud and others in psychoanalysis.

References

Aru J, Bachmann T, Singer W, Melloni L (2012) Distilling the neural correlates of consciousness. Neurosci Biobehav Rev. 36:737–746. https://doi.org/10.1016/j.neubiorev.2011.12.003

Baria AT, Maniscalco B, He BJ (2017) Initial-state-dependent, robust, transient neural dynamics encode conscious visual perception. PLoS Computational Biology. 13:e1005806. https://doi.org/10.1371/journal.pcbi.1005806

Bazan A (2012) From sensorimotor inhibition to Freudian repression: Insights from psychosis applied to neurosis. Front Psychol. Nov 5;3:452. doi: 10.3389/fpsyg.2012.00452. eCollection 2012.

Bazan A (2017) Alpha synchronization as a brain model for unconscious defense: An overview of the work of Howard Shevrin and his team. Int J Psychoanal. Oct;98(5):1443–1473. doi: 10.1111/1745-8315.12629. Epub 2017 Mar 1.

Benswell CSY, Tagliabue CF, Veniero D, Cecere R, Savazzi S, Thut G (2017) Prestimulus EEG power predicts conscious awareness but not objective visual performance. eNeuro. 4. https://doi.org/10.1523/ENEURO.0182-17.2017

Block N (2005) Two neural correlates of consciousness. Trends in Cognitive Sciences. 9:46–52. https://doi.org/10.1016/j.tics.2004.12.006

Chalmers D (1996) The conscious mind. Oxford University Press, Oxford, New York.

de Graaf TA, Hsieh PJ, Sack AT (2012) The "correlates" in neural correlates of consciousness. Neurosci Biobehav Rev. Jan;36(1):191–197. doi: 10.1016/j.neubiorev.2011.05.012. Epub 2011 Jun 1.

Dijk H van, Schoffelen J-M, Oostenveld R, Jensen O (2008) Prestimulus oscillatory activity in the alpha band predicts visual discrimination ability. J. Neurosci. 28:1816–1823. https://doi.org/10.1523/JNEUROSCI.1853-07.2008

Freud S (1915) The unconscious (SE, Vol. 14, pp. 166–204). Hogarth Press, London.

Golesorkhi M, Gomez-Pilar J, Tumati S, Fraser M, Northoff G (2021a) Temporal hierarchy of intrinsic neural timescales converges with spatial core-periphery organization. Commun Biol. Mar 4;4(1):277. doi: 10.1038/s42003-021-01785-z

Golesorkhi M, Gomez-Pilar J, Zilio F, Berberian N, Wolff A, Yagoub MCE, Northoff G (2021b) The brain and its time: Intrinsic neural timescales are key for input processing. Commun Biol. Aug 16;4(1):970. doi: 10.1038/s42003-021-02483-6

Hesselmann G, Kell CA, Eger E, Kleinschmidt A (2008) Spontaneous local variations in ongoing neural activity bias perceptual decisions. PNAS. 105:10984–10989. https://doi.org/10.1073/pnas.0712043105

Hua J, Zhang Y, Wolff A, Northoff G (2021) Thought dynamics is mediated by alpha and theta peak frequency. Nature Communication Biology, in press.

Huang Z, Zhang J, Longtin A, Dumont G, Duncan NW, Pokorny J, Qin P, Dai R, Ferri F, Weng X, Northoff G (2017) Is there a nonadditive interaction between spontaneous and evoked activity? Phase-dependence and its relation to the temporal structure of scale-free brain activity. Cereb Cortex. 27:1037–1059. https://doi.org/10.1093/cercor/bhv288

Hudetz AG, Liu X, Pillay S (2015) Dynamic repertoire of intrinsic brain states is reduced in propofol-induced unconsciousness. Brain Connect. 5:10–22. https://doi.org/10.1089/brain.2014.0230

Kihlstroem J (1987) The cognitive unconscious. Science. 237:1445–1452

Kihlstroem JE, Barnhardt T, Tataryn D (1992) The psychological unconscious: Found, lost and regained. American Psychologist. 47(6):788–791.

Koch C (2004) Consciousness. Oxford University Press, Oxford, New York.

Koch C, Massimini M, Boly M, Tononi G (2016) Neural correlates of consciousness: Progress and problems. Nat. Rev. Neurosci. 17:307–321. https://doi.org/10.1038/nrn.2016.22

Lamme VAF (2018) Challenges for theories of consciousness: Seeing or knowing, the missing ingredient and how to deal with panpsychism. Phil. Trans. R. Soc. B 373:20170344. https://doi.org/10.1098/rstb.2017.0344

Lau H, Rosenthal D (2011) Empirical support for higher-order theories of conscious awareness. Trends Cogn Sci. Aug;15(8):365–373. doi: 10.1016/j.tics.2011.05.009. Epub 2011 Jul 6.

Mashour GA, Roelfsema P, Changeux JP, Dehaene S (2020) Conscious processing and the global neuronal workspace hypothesis. Neuron. Mar 4;105(5):776–798. doi: 10.1016/j.neuron.2020.01.026

Nagel T (1998) Conceiving the impossible and the mind-body problem. Philosophy. 73:337–352.

Northoff G (2018) The spontaneous brain: From the mind-body to the world-brain problem. MIT Press, Cambridge, MA.

Northoff G, Heiss WD (2015) Why is the distinction between neural predispositions, prerequisites, and correlates of the level of consciousness clinically relevant?: Functional brain imaging in coma and vegetative state. Stroke. Apr;46(4):1147–1151. doi: 10.1161/STROKEAHA.114.007969. Epub 2015 Feb 10.

Northoff G, Huang Z (2017) How do the brain's time and space mediate consciousness and its different dimensions? Temporo-spatial theory of consciousness (TTC). Neurosci Biobehav Rev. 80:630–645. https://doi.org/10.1016/j.neubiorev.2017.07.013

Northoff G, Lamme V (2020) Neural signs and mechanisms of consciousness: Is there a potential convergence of theories of consciousness in sight? Neurosci Biobehav Rev. Nov;118:568–587. doi: 10.1016/j.neubiorev.2020.07.019. Epub 2020 Aug 9.

Northoff G, Wainio-Theberge S, Evers K (2020a) Is temporo-spatial dynamics the "common currency" of brain and mind? In quest of "spatiotemporal neuroscience". Phys Life Rev. Jul;33:34–54. doi: 10.1016/j.plrev.2019.05.002. Epub 2019 May 23.

Northoff G, Wainio-Theberge S, Evers K (2020b) Spatiotemporal neuroscience: What is it and why we need it. Phys Life Rev. Jul;33:78–87. doi: 10.1016/j.plrev.2020.06.005. Epub 2020 Jul 10.

Northoff G, Zilio F (2021) Temporo-spatial theory of consciousness (TTC): From neuronal to phenomenal features. Behavioral Brain Research. in press.

Panksepp J (1998) Affective neuroscience. Oxford University Press, Oxford, New York.

Panksepp J, Biven L (2012) The archaeology of mind. Norton Publisher, New York.

Podvalny E, Flounders MW, King LE, Holroyd T, He BJ (2019) A dual role of prestimulus spontaneous neural activity in visual object recognition. Nature Communications. 10:1–13. https://doi.org/10.1038/s41467-019-11877-4

Romei V, Gross J, Thut G (2010) On the role of prestimulus alpha rhythms over occipito-parietal areas in visual input regulation: Correlation or causation? J. Neurosci. 30:8692–8697. https://doi.org/10.1523/JNEUROSCI.0160-10.2010

Sadaghiani S, Hesselmann G, Friston KJ, Kleinschmidt A (2010) The relation of ongoing brain activity, evoked neural responses, and cognition. Front Syst Neurosci. 4. https://doi.org/10.3389/fnsys.2010.00020

Sadaghiani S, Poline J-B, Kleinschmidt A, D'Esposito M (2015) Ongoing dynamics in large-scale functional connectivity predict perception. PNAS. 112:8463–8468. https://doi.org/10.1073/pnas.1420687112

Schuessler G (2002) Aktuelle Konzepte des Unbewussten. Zeitschrift fuer Psychosomatische Medizin und Psychotherapy. 48:192–214.

Shevrin H, Snodgrass M, Brakel LA, Kushwaha R, Kalaida NL, Bazan A (2013) Subliminal unconscious conflict alpha power inhibits supraliminal conscious symptom experience. Front Hum Neurosci. Sep 5;7:544. doi: 10.3389/fnhum.2013.00544. eCollection 2013.

Solms M (2015) The feeling brain. Routledge, London, New York.

Solms M (2019) The hard problem of consciousness and the free energy principle. Front Psychology. Jan 30;9:2714. doi: 10.3389/fpsyg.2018.02714. eCollection 2018.

Tononi G, Boly M, Massimini M, Koch C (2016) Integrated information theory: From consciousness to its physical substrate. Nature Reviews Neuroscience. 17:450–461. https://doi.org/10.1038/nrn.2016.44

Uleman JS (2005) Introduction: Becoming aware of the new unconscious. In: The unconscious (pp. 1–12), G Hassin, JS Uleman. MIT Press, Cambridge, MA.

Vanhaudenhuyse A, Demertzi A, Schabus M, Noirhomme Q, Bredart S, Boly M, Phillips C, Soddu A, Luxen A, Moonen G, Laureys SJ (2011) Two distinct neuronal networks mediate the awareness of environment and of self. Cogn Neurosci. Mar;23(3):570–578. doi: 10.1162/jocn.2010.21488. Epub 2010 Jun 1.

Wolff A, Yao L, Gomez-Pilar J, Shoaran M, Jiang N, Northoff G (2019) Neural variability quenching during decision-making: Neural individuality and its prestimulus complexity. Neuroimage. 192:1–14. https://doi.org/10.1016/j.neuroimage.2019.02.070

Zhang J, Huang Z, Tumati S, Northoff G (2020) Rest-task modulation of fMRI-derived global signal topography is mediated by transient coactivation patterns. PLoS Biol. July 10;18(7):e3000733. doi: 10.1371/journal.pbio.3000733. eCollection 2020 July.

Zhang J, Magioncalda P, Huang Z, Tan Z, Hu X, Hu Z, Conio B, Amore M, Inglese M, Martino M, Northoff G (2019) Altered global signal topography and its different regional localization in motor cortex and hippocampus in mania and depression. Schizophr Bull. Jun 18;45(4):902–910. doi: 10.1093/schbul/sby138

Chapter 6

Dreams

Introduction

Dreams take on a key role in psychoanalysis. They provide access to the unconscious, that is, the "via regia to the unconscious". At the same time, dreams are considered therapeutic, as they offer insight into early traumatic memories that then can be used for conflict resolution in psychotherapy. Finally, there has been much neuroscientific research on dreams in recent years so that they provide a paradigmatic example of inner mental life.

Going back to Freud, dreams are psychoanalytically often conceived as wish fulfillment reflecting endogenous drives and primary processes that are disinhibited and uncontrolled. They are conceived as the hallucinatory realization of those impulses that are strongly driven by energy, that is, cathexis, and unconscious affective demands. More recently, dreams have been related to specific affect/emotions like the SEEKING system that drives emotion and behavior (Panksepp and Biven 2012; Solms 2020), while cognitively, dreams are associated with unconscious memories: the memories often can be traced back to early childhood where they have been "stored" in terms of body signatures in the unconscious without yet leaving any cognitive traces in the conscious. Consecutively, the concept of "embodied memories" has been invoked to describe those memories that are recruited and reactivated during dreams (Leuzinger-Bohleber et al. 2019).

DOI: 10.4324/9781003132905-7

The study of dreams has gone far beyond psychoanalysis to psychology and neuroscience in recent years, though. Hence, some of the original psychodynamic features of dreams like unconscious memories are now taken up in psychology and neuroscience. I suppose that the topography and dynamic of the psyche (first part) during dreams is manifest in a more or less corresponding topography and dynamic of the brain (second part). That leads me to develop what I describe as the "topographic-dynamic re-organization theory of dreams" (TRoD) (third part).

Part I: topography and dynamic of the *psyche* in dreams

Dream contents I – semantic association vs semantic similarity/identity of external contents

Psychologically, dreams can first and foremost be characterized by rather bizarre emotions and cognitions in the hallucinatory episodes. Contents that are usually not connected or integrated are now linked and combined or put together in a semantically novel way. One can still somewhat identify certain familiar external environmental contents like other humans, buildings, and so on, but they are put together in a semantically bizarre and strange way. Hence, there is some semantic connection between the conscious contents in the awake state and those occurring during dreams.

However, that connection does not imply semantic identity or sameness of the external contents in awake and dream states. Fogel et al. (2018) developed a particular method to investigate the degree of semantic association during dreams. They let subjects, during the awake state, mentally imagine tennis playing (after seeing real tennis players in visual display) (and spatially navigate) in the awake state. After that, they asked the subjects to take short naps from which they were woken up asked to report their dreams. The investigators recorded all the words and sentences uttered by the subjects in their dream reports; their dream reports were then entered into a machine learning algorithm for detecting semantic relations to tennis playing (and spatial navigation). This allowed researchers to detect and quantify the degree to which semantic contents associated with tennis were incorporated into the contents experienced during dreams.

The results show that there is a semantic relationship of the dream contents with tennis playing. For instance, the subjects dreamt about playing ball on the green lane in a park but did not experience tennis playing itself. This suggests semantic association but not semantic similarity: the contents during the awake state (tennis) were incorporated into the dream contents (soccer playing in a park) but were not replayed in an identical or similar way. Hence, there is semantic association but not semantic similarity or identity.

This is well in accordance with, for instance, the paintings by Salvador Dali. He reconstructed his often bizarre dream contents in his paintings: they are bizarre because they reflect distortions and thus semantic associations of the real contents occurring in the awake state. Dreams are thus not simply a replay of semantically similar contents. Instead, they feature active manipulation of our awake contents during the dream state.

Dream contents II – manipulation of internal contents like body, emotion, memories, and self

We have so far focused only on externally oriented mental contents like the tennis playing in dreams. The active manipulation of dreams extends even further, as it also includes mental contents of internally oriented cognition and emotion. The best example of that is the experience of the own body and its self in dreams. As in the case of our tennis example, the relationship of body and self in dreams is somewhat loosened but not disrupted during dreams. For instance, the own body may no longer be experienced as such – rather, as in extreme cases, one may experience oneself to be out of one's own body, something that is described as "full body illusion" (FBI) (Windt 2021).

Despite being possibly detached from its own body, the own self is still experienced as such at the same time. It is after all my own self in first-person perspective that experiences the contents in the dream hallucination – this experience of the own self has been described as "felt presence" (FP) (Windt 2021). Hence, even if "body-less", dreams are not "self-less". The presence of self is even more supported by the fact that dream contents are highly autobiographical.

As pointed out in psychodynamics, dream contents tell us about the own self and its hidden and/or earlier experiences that remain unconscious in the awake state. Dreams may thus be seen as an entrance gate to the dynamic unconscious and possibly also, in part, of the deep unconscious of the self: this may be manifest in the self's previous relations to the environment which, usually remaining unconscious in the awake state, resurface in dreams.

The experience of an altered sense of self and its otherwise unconscious life events is accompanied by strong affects and emotions in dreams. They mostly reflect what Panksepp describes as primary emotions, seeking, lust, care, and so on, which psychodynamically can be described as primary processes (Panksepp and Biven 2012; Solms 2015, 2020, 2021). Especially the SEEKING system, which drives emotion and behavior, has been assumed to take on a key role in dreams (Panksepp and Biven 2012; Solms 2020).

Importantly, the affects and emotions in dreams are often described as unbound, free-floating, and unconstrained, remaining devoid of any form of rationality. The same may apply to certain cognitive contents like the events one experiences in dreams that may also be more or less free-floating proceeding in a completely spontaneous way without any deliberative control (Christoff et al. 2016; Windt 2021; Fox et al. 2016). One can thus characterize affect not only by its often bizarre nature in dreams but also by its extreme degree of spontaneity, lacking any containment by deliberative and rational control. This suggests that the dynamic of dreams is also changing compared to the awake state.

Besides their strong affects/emotions, dreams also involve unconscious memories: the memories often can be traced back to early childhood where they have been "stored" in terms of body signatures in the unconscious without yet leaving any cognitive traces in the conscious. Consecutively, the concept of "embodied memories" has been invoked to describe memories recruited and reactivated during dreams (Leuzinger-Bohleber et al. 2019).

The psyche and its dreams – topography and dynamic

Together, these phenomenological observations clearly point out an active dream-related manipulation of the contents of both externally and internally oriented contents. Both the external environment (external events in awake state) and the internal self with its body and emotions are experienced in a distorted way. However, they can still be recognized as such but are different – there is semantic association rather than semantic similarity/identity.

Put in more psychodynamic terms, dreams are paradigmatic examples of an altered topography of the psyche. We need to distinguish between content and topography, with the latter describing the context in which the former are processed during both awake and dream states. We postulate that the context; that is, the topography changes during dreams. Now the same content, that is, that of the awake state, is replayed during dreams in a different topographic context – this, as we suppose, changes the content. Rather than simulating, e.g., replaying the awake contents in an identical way, the awake contents are now embedded in an altered overall mental topography: the contents from the awake state are manipulated by their changed topographical context, for which reason they remain only semantically related but not identical to the original awake contents.

Where and how are such changes in the topography of the psyche during dreams coming from? This leads us to the topography and dynamic of the brain and specifically how they change during dreams compared to awake states. Following the assumption of "common currency" with shared features of mental and neural states (Northoff et al. 2020a, 2020b), we suppose that the altered topography and dynamic of the psyche during dreams is related to more or less analogous changes in the topography and dynamic of the brain.

Part II: topography and dynamic of the *brain* in dreams

Topography of the cortex in dreams I – default-mode network, hippocampus, and visual cortex

One cannot conceive the brain's topographic changes in REM sleep, which is associated with strong dreams independent of the other sleep stages. The NREM 1 sleep stage is characterized by mostly activation in visual cortex and its various widespread regions. At the same time, it seems that the lateral prefrontal cortex and the central executive network (CEN) tend to reduce their activity level at this stage (Tanabe et al. 2020). NREM 2 shows more diffuse changes, which are not yet clearly identified, as the results are rather confusing, if not contradictory (Fox et al. 2016; Tanabe et al. 2020).

Finally, the slow-wave sleep stages, NREM 3 and 4, show generally reduced activity levels in widespread regions of the brain with lower degrees of functional connectivity between all regions (Tanabe et al. 2020). We need to be careful, though, as these results are based on a limited number of studies due to the difficulties of conducting fMRI in different sleep stages.

More studies are available for REM sleep. Here the patterns show increased activation and connectivity of medial temporal regions like the hippocampus. Given that the hippocampus is key in encoding and retrieving memory, this fits well with the observation that memories are increasingly recruited or retrieved during dreams as well as, at the same time, enhanced after a dream-rich sleep. Additionally, there is increased activity and connectivity within the cortical midline regions of the DMN in especially the medial prefrontal cortex, while, at the same time, activity in lateral prefrontal cortex and CEN is reduced. Hence, the reciprocal modulation of medial vs lateral prefrontal and, more generally, between DMN and CEN, is shifted towards the DMN in dreams.

Finally, there is also increased activity in widespread regions of the visual cortex during dreams, that is, REM, compared to NREM sleep stages (Fox et al. 2013; Domhoff and Fox 2015; Fox et al. 2013, 2016). This is even more remarkable given that the eyes are closed during sleep so that the subjects do not receive direct visual input from the external environment. The observed activity increase in the visual cortex may consequently be related to internal (rather than external) input from the visual cortex's own spontaneous activity. Together, the visual cortex's resting state activity is elevated in dreams.

In contrast, task-evoked activity in the visual cortex, as usually associated with external visual inputs, remains absent due to the lack of visual processing of external environmental inputs (eyes are closed). The increase in visual cortex resting state activity during dreams may reach the level that the visual cortex usually displays in the awake state when processing external visual inputs. During dreams subjects may thus take their elevated spontaneous visual cortex activity to be indicative of events occurring in the external environment (see Northoff and Qin 2011 for an analogous case in auditory cortex during auditory hallucination in schizophrenia). This is well in accordance with dream experience where subjects often report external environmental scenes and events, albeit in a distorted way.

Together, these findings suggest that REM sleep is characterized by a distinct cortical topography compared to both the awake state and NREM sleep (see also Qin et al. 2021). The reciprocal DMN-CEN balance is shifted towards the DMN, with a reduced activity level in CEN. Moreover, medial temporal regions, including the hippocampus, seem to show elevated activity. Finally, the visual cortex, despite the closed eyes with a lack of external visual input, is elevated in its spontaneous activity. Accordingly, putting it all together, the spatial topography of the dreaming (REM) brain is distinct from those during both awake and other sleep (NREM) states.

Topography of the cortex in dreams II – subcortical–cortical biochemical modulation

Why and how is there such a change in the brain's topography during dreams? One possibility is that the topography of the cortex is modulated in a different way by the subcortical nuclei of different biochemical systems.

Biochemically, subcortically originating cortical neuromodulatory transmitter systems like acetylcholine (forebrain – nucleus basalis of Meynert), dopamine (ventral tegmental area and substantia nigra), serotonin (raphe nucleus), and adrenalin/noradrenalin (locus coerulus) have been associated with changes in sleep (compared to awake). Moreover, they show differential changes in NREM and REM sleep, making it likely that dreams are mediated by a particular subcortical biochemical signature with respect to acetylcholine, dopamine, serotonin, and adrenaline/noradrenaline (Fox et al. 2013). The concentrations of these transmitters are in somewhat of an intermediate level in REM sleep between higher concentrations in the awake state and lower ones in NREM.

However, it shall be noticed that it is not one particular transmitter system and one subcortical region but rather their balance that seems to be specifically altered in dreams. There seems to be a relative increase in acetylcholine and dopamine (relative to serotonin and adrenaline/noradrenaline) in REM that may be key for dreams. This is supported by the known impact of acetylcholine and its nucleus basalis of Meynert on the level of arousal/consciousness (Fox et al. 2013; Zhang et al. 2020; Zhang and Northoff 2021; Tanabe et al. 2020).

Most interestingly, these subcortical nuclei and their respective transmitters modulate cortical patterns in a global way (Zhang et al. 2020; Conio et al. 2020). For instance, they modulate the balance between DMN and sensorimotor networks as well as between DMN and salience network (that includes the insula) (Conio et al. 2020). Changes on the cortical level and its topography may thus, in part, be related to the shifts in their subcortical–cortical biochemical modulation.

Together, dreams are characterized by changes in subcortical–cortical biochemical modulation with shifts between different biochemicals. Can such a change in subcortical–cortical modulation account for the shift towards subcortically driven primary emotions like SEEKING, drives, and predominant primary processes in dreams? At the same time, can it also explain the loss of the more cortically mediated rational and intentional control, including their secondary processes? To address these questions, we shift our focus to the dynamics of the brain in dreams.

Dynamic of the cortex in dreams I – shift to slower frequencies

Dynamic can be measured using EEG for the temporal dynamics of the power spectrum and various electrophysiological changes. NREM 1 sleep is typically characterized by a decrease of alpha (8–13 Hz) combined with the strengthening of power and occurrence of ripple waves in theta (5–8 Hz). NREM 2 features high frequency spindles (12–30 Hz) and large-amplitude K-complexes. Finally, NREM 3 and 4 show highly synchronized slow waves (0.5 to 4 Hz).

REM sleep shows highly desynchronized low amplitude activity in EEG in mainly theta (5–8 Hz) and beta (13–30 Hz), which resemble the awake state; the difference is that REM sleep lacks the alpha power that characterizes the awake state. The alpha power is typically decreased, while theta power is relatively increased during dreams (see also Berberian et al. 2022). That is also reflected in the power law exponent that, measuring the balance of slow and fast frequency power, is lower in dreams compared to NREM 2 and 3 but still higher than in the awake state. The dream state is thus characterized by more power in the slow frequencies relative to faster ones when compared to the awake state, while it is still faster than deep sleep (N3) (Zilio et al. 2021).

Dynamic of the cortex in dreams II – longer time windows

The intermediate position of REM sleep between awake and deep sleep (N3) is also reflected in its intrinsic neural timescales (INT). REM sleep shows shorter intrinsic neural timescales than NREM as measured by the autocorrelation window (ACW): the ACW in dreams is shorter than in N2 and N3 but still longer than in the awake state (Zilio et al. 2021). The ACW and, more generally, the INT are important in processing input, as they parse the input streams into different chunks through temporal integration and segregation (Golesorkhi et al. 2021a, 2021b). Longer temporal windows (longer ACWs) favor the temporal integration of different inputs both internally and externally while, at the same time, diminishing their temporal segregation (Wolff et al. 2022).

This leads us to the following tentative hypothesis. The longer temporal windows, together with the shift towards slower frequencies, may explain why different "normal" contents are put together in an abnormal way: temporally distinct contents may be summed or lumped together in dreams, that is, high temporal integration, which otherwise, as in the awake state, may be separated, that is, higher temporal segregation, given its shorter time windows and faster frequencies. The typically bizarre dream contents may thus, in part, be related to the shift towards temporal integration of inputs at the expense of temporal segregation which, neuronally, may be related to the shift towards longer time windows and slower frequencies. One would consequently hypothesize that the degree of semantic association as distinguished from semantic identity/similarity should be related to the degree to which temporal integration becomes stronger over temporal segregation in dreams compared to awake. That, in turn, should be related to the degree of prolongation of the brain's INT, that is, its ACW.

Part III: topographic-dynamic reorganization theory of dreams

Given the findings of an altered topography and dynamic of the brain, we now aim to link the brain's neuronal level to the psychological dreams of dreams. Specifically, we suggest that the altered topography and dynamic of the brain are manifest in more analogous topography and dynamic of the psyche. This amounts to what I here, for the first time, introduce as the topographic-dynamic reorganization theory of dreams. The background assumption of TRoD is that topographic and dynamic changes are shared in a more or less corresponding way by both brain and psyche as their "common currency" (Northoff et al. 2020a, 2020b).

Topographic reorganization – increase in internally oriented cognition

Dreams are characterized by topographic reorganization of the cortex. One key feature is that the balance of DMN-CEN shifts towards the DMN. The CEN and especially the lateral prefrontal cortex are related to cognitive control and goal orientation. These are strongly diminished in dreams, where rational and voluntary control are lost, while spontaneity and automatic involuntary dynamic of affect/emotion and cognition/thought are strongly increased. One would thus hypothesize that the loss of rational voluntary control and goal orientation with respect to emotions and cognition are related to the relative decrease of CEN activity in dreams. This remains to be tested in the future.

How about the DMN? The data show that DMN activity is relatively increased in dreams. The DMN is well known to mediate internally oriented cognition like mental time travel, autobiographical memory, and mind-wandering (Christoff et al. 2016; Fox et al. 2016). All three are increased in dreams: there is indeed mental time travel, with abnormal shifts towards either the past or future accompanied by detachment from the present, that is, the actual point in time. Autobiographical memories are increasingly retrieved during dreams – this may be especially related to increased hippocampal activity. Finally, there is increased mind-wandering with freely floating unconstrained thoughts in dreams.

Albeit tentatively, one may hypothesize that the changes in these three forms of internally oriented cognition may, in part, be related to the abnormal increase in DMN activity, including the hippocampus. Moreover, the increases in both DMN and its internally oriented cognition during dreams may provide an access to the dynamic unconscious (Chapter 5). For that reason, dreams are often conceived as taking on a key role in psychodynamic psychotherapy (Leuzinger-Bohleber et al. 2019).

The topographic shift towards DMN goes along with a dynamic shift towards slower frequencies and longer time windows in the brain's neural activity during dreams. Are topographic and dynamic changes related to each other? We currently do not know. We know, though, that, in the awake state, the DMN exhibits slower frequencies and longer time windows than CEN and especially unimodal sensory regions (Golesorkhi et al. 2021a, 2021b). Inferring from these findings in the awake state, one may assume that the topographic shift towards DMN during dreams goes along with a dynamic shift towards slower frequencies and longer time windows. These dynamic changes, in turn, may favor internally oriented cognition, as that is known to be related to slow dynamic and long timescales (Vanhaudenhuyse et al. 2011; Hua et al. 2021).

Self in dreams I – relative increase of the mental self

The awake state is characterized by a topography of self marked by its nestedness of three layers of self (Chapter 1 and Qin et al. 2020). Roughly, interoceptive self, featuring the own inner body, is the lowest layer, being related to the insula and subcortical regions. That is followed by the proprioceptive self that extends to the outer body as mediated by additional regions like temporo-parietal junction. Finally, the third most upper layer consists in the mental self that is mediated by the DMN and especially its midline structure (see Chapter 1 for details as well as Qin et al. 2020).

How is this three-layer nestedness of the self affected in dreams? The topographic shifts in subcortical and cortical regions during dreams strongly suggest that the three-layer nested hierarchy of self is also shifted and rebalanced. The increase in DMN suggests an increase in the mental self while, due to the lacking extero- and proprioceptive input, the middle layer of the proprioceptive self may be relatively diminished during dreams. Psychologically, the increase of mental self may be related to what is described as the "felt presence" of self: this describes an increased presence of the own self in one's mental states, that is, mental self, during dreams (Windt 2021).

The increased presence of the mental self in dreams is further supported by the dynamic changes. In the awake state, more powerful slow frequencies and longer time windows in DMN activity are known to mediate higher degrees of self-consciousness (Huang et al. 2016; Wolff et al. 2019; Kolvoort et al. 2020). The shift towards slower frequencies and longer timescales during dreams may thus translate into an increased mental self: the increased power of the slower frequencies may be manifest psychologically in the experience of a more powerful self that is increasingly present in one's experience and mental states.

Self in dreams II – relative decrease of the proprioceptive self

The self is not limited to the mental self, though. The increase in mental self may go along with a relative decrease of the proprioceptive self as mediated by the TPJ. In the awake state, the TPJ is well known to mediate out-of-body experiences even in healthy subjects (Blanke et al. 2015). Inferring again from the awake state, one would thus assume that the typical occurrence of partial- or full-body illusions with, in the most extreme instances, out-of-body experiences during dreams (Windt 2021) may be related to the (relative) activity decrease of the TPJ and other regions constituting the middle layer of the proprioceptive self. Hence, while the DMN and its mental self are increasingly present in dreams, the proprioceptive self and its neural correlates may be diminished (in at least a relative way).

Neuronally, one would expect decoupling of insula and subcortical regions (interoceptive self) and TPJ (exteroceptive self) from the DMN (mental self) – their degree of connectivity and ultimately their degree of nestedness may decrease in dreams, resulting in the experience of a mental self detached from its own body's intero- and proprio-exteroceptive input. The upper layer of the mental self and its DMN may consequently be less nested and contained within the lower layers of the intero- and exteroceptive self as related to subcortical and cortical regions like the thalamus, insula, and TPJ.

Self in dreams III – relative increase of the interoceptive self

Finally, these topographical changes on the cortical level may, in part, be driven by subcortical sources and their various transmitter systems. Subcortically located transmitter systems like serotonine, noradrenaline, acetylcholine, dopamine, and others (Fox et al. 2013) are changing during sleep in general and also in dreams, where they seem to show peculiar shifts in their balances. Since subcortical regions in pons, brainstem, and forebrain like the raphe nucleus (serotonin) and the nucleus basalis of Meynert (acetylcholine) mediate cortical balance of DMN, CEN, and other non-DMN networks (Conio et al. 2020; Martino et al. 2020), changes in the cortical topography in both its spatial and temporal aspects may be related, in part, to these subcortical shifts in the balances of different transmitter systems.

Do these subcortical changes translate into a relative increase in the interoceptive self and thus the bodily based self during dreams? The bodily or interoceptive self may be decoupled from and less nested within the mental self. This may be manifest in the decrease of voluntary control of the interoceptive self by the mental self: this may be related to the increased spontaneity and involuntary automaticity with the increased occurrence of drives, primary processes and primary affects/emotions like SEEKING, as is typical for dreams (Panksepp and Biven 2012). Together, one would assume that the subcortical–cortical changes during dreams may be related to a relative increase of the interoceptive self, while, at the same time, the interoceptive self is increasingly detached from and less nested within the more upper layers of the proprioceptive and especially mental self.

Spatiotemporal reference frame I – immersive spatiotemporal hallucination

Why are the experiences in dreams so bizarre and, at the same time, somewhat familiar, though? We still have the experience to navigate in some kind of environment during dreams, albeit in a distorted way. Jennifer Windt (Windt 2010, 2021; Windt and Noreika 2011) proposes that there is still a spatiotemporal reference framework in place during dreams for the presence of self, full-body illusions, and environmental experiences. She therefore proposes to describe dreams as "immersive spatiotemporal hallucination" (ISTH). ISTH are described as amodal manifestations of hallucinations concerning both internally and externally oriented cognition, which, during dreams, operate within an abnormal spatiotemporal reference framework.

We hallucinate in dreams about the external environment, including our own self as part of it, even though we are more or less detached and decoupled from the external environmental input. The lack of external environmental input seems to be compensated for by the relative increase of internal inputs from within both body and brain themselves during dreams. In addition to the more interoceptive sources from the body, this internal input may come from within the brain itself most notably the DMN and visual cortex (VC), which are strongly activated during dreams (see previously).

Together, this links the DMN-based internal inputs that are internally oriented in their contents with the VC-based internal inputs that are usually externally oriented in their contents (as it comes from visual cortex usually mediating external environmental contents). That, as I propose, constitutes a spatiotemporal reference framework, probably in a three-dimensional (or multi-dimensional) way, within which the various types of contents are perceived and experienced in an abnormal way, that is, semantically associated but not semantically similar.

Spatiotemporal reference frame II – semantic association rather than semantic similarity

One may be confused by the distinction of internal vs external inputs relative to internally vs externally oriented contents. The brain and especially the visual cortex are isolated from direct external input in dreams: the eyes are closed, which blocks external visual input from the environment. However, the visual cortex still exhibits neural activity, that is, spontaneous activity during dreams independent of any direct external input. This spontaneous activity thus provides an internal input to the visual cortex.

However, since the visual cortex is usually associated with external input and its externally oriented cognition contents, the internal input is now processed as if it were an external input: it is consequently associated with externally oriented cognition contents (see also Vanhaudenhuyse et al. 2011): "the brain isolated from the outside world, treats its endogenous stimulation as if it were exogenous" (Hobson 2009, 809). This, according to Hobson (2009, 808), leads the dreamer to make or "built-in predictions about external time and space". Due to the peculiar combination of internal input and externally oriented cognition contents, I characterized dreams by "as if external perception" and "as if objects" in my earlier book (Northoff 2011, 196ff).

Moreover, the VC-based constitution and prediction of external time and space allows linking it to the internal space and time predictions as related to the DMN and the self (Northoff et al. 2018 for the distinction of inner/internal and outer/external time and space). Together, the connection of DMN and VC mediating internal and external time-space allows to constitute a virtual spatiotemporal reference frame during dreams just as in the awake state. The difference is only that the spatiotemporal reference frames in dreams and awake exhibit distinct coordinates, that is, a different spatiotemporal organization or topography. I therefore speak of topographical reorganization of the spatiotemporal reference frame in dreams.

This is supported by a recent paper by Berberian et al. (2022). They demonstrate that the shift towards slower frequencies like theta peak frequency is directly related to the degree of semantic association: the stronger the theta peak frequency, the higher the degree to which the awake scenario, that is, spatial navigation, is incorporated into the semantic meaning of dreams during naps. Hence, the same content, that is, spatial navigation, is now processed in a different dynamic context, that is, slower as related to theta rather than alpha peak frequency (Berberian et al. 2022). The changes in the brain's dynamic or temporal reference framework during dreams thus shifts the semantic meaning of the same contents.

Such a reorganized spatiotemporal reference frame harbors and embeds the various contents in dreams in a way different form their embedding in the awake state: the "normal" contents themselves become embedded and integrated with an abnormal and "distorted" spatiotemporal reference frame. For instance, one and the same input like an interoceptive input from the body or a neuronal input from visual cortex is now processed in the context of a topography shifted towards DMN and a dynamic characterized by slow frequencies and longer time windows. That, in turn, "distorts" the meaning of the content – the contents in dreams are still the same, but their meaning or semantics shifts and therefore remains no longer exactly the same. This may account for what we described previously as semantic association as distinguished from both semantic non-association/ difference and semantic similarity/identity. That is well compatible with the depiction of the often bizarre backgrounds in Salvador Dali's paintings that "distort" the contents in the foreground.

Conclusion – from dreams and TRoD to psychotherapy

Dreams provide the via regia to the unconscious. That is literally true, as they operate on a deeper layer of the psyche than the awake state. Since they operate on this deeper layer, their effects can reverberate to the upper layers and reorganize them – this allows for what psychotherapists describe as "structural change". Taken within the context of the TRoD, such "structural change" is topographic (and dynamic) change that can be traced to the reorganization of the brain's topography and its dynamic. The TRoD claims that such topographic and dynamic changes in the brain are manifest in analogous ways on the mental level accounting for semantic association, hallucination, and changes in body and self during dreams.

I now extend the TRoD to the realm of psychotherapy, which can be viewed as therapy of the topographical and dynamic organization of both brain and psyche. One key focus of psychotherapy are traumatic events for whose resolution dreams are used as therapeutic tools. Due to the topographic reorganization, the problematic or traumatic event or content, as originally situated in the dynamic unconscious, may now gain access to a wider spatiotemporal repertoire during dreams: this concerns the different topography with more subcortical–cortical bottom-up modulation and less DMN-top-down modulation as well as changed dynamic with slower frequencies.

This topographic and dynamic reorganization may make possible to more easily access the traumatic events of the dynamic unconscious as well as to integrate them with other non-traumatic events as "the more 'healthy' parts of the unconscious and conscious". Traumatic events are thus linked to and integrated within non-traumatic events (of the "healthy" parts of the self) through spatiotemporal integration, that is, topographic and dynamic integration, into a novel and possibly wider spatiotemporal context. That, in turn, mitigates the effects of the traumatic event that now can find its passage from the dynamic unconscious over the preconscious to the conscious.

Neuronally, I hypothesize that this wider opening of the unconscious–conscious passage may be related neuronally to especially the changes in the degree of temporo-spatial nestedness among the three layers of self during dreams: the mental self exerts less top-down control, which releases the interoceptive self, allowing it increased spontaneity which, as we assume, facilitates and releases the dynamic unconscious, including its more embodied memories of the traumatic events.

What does this imply for psychotherapy? The therapist may want to analyze dreams primarily in spatiotemporal terms rather than exclusively focusing on the contents themselves: the relation between the different contents, their spatial configuration, and temporal changes over time should be the main focus. Dreams are consequently no longer analyzed primarily in a content-based way, including both affective and cognitive contents. Instead, the integration of the affective and cognitive contents into a spatiotemporal framework as subjectively perceived and experienced by the subjects may be key in psychotherapy.

There are limits to what the subjects can report of their dreams, though. Besides verbal report, one can include non-verbal report like painting or drawing (just like Salvador Dali did): the spatiotemporal coordinates of the drawings may then provide some insight into the spatiotemporal reference frame of the dream itself, which, in turn, may mirror the spatiotemporal dynamic repertoire of the brain itself (see Lin et al. 2020 for a first investigation).

The psychotherapist may then work spatiotemporally with the client in order to reset her/his spatiotemporal reference frame. That could, for instance, be done by modulating the frequency and speed of the own language, the spatial interaction with the client, and various other ways. Ideally, that is accompanied by continuous monitoring of the client's brain states using brain-computer interface which will show on-line how the therapeutic or better spatiotemporal intervention by the therapist modulates the client's spatiotemporal dynamic repertoire. Dynamic psychotherapy of dreams may thus transform into what can be described as "spatiotemporal psychotherapy" (see Spagnioli and Northoff 2021; Northoff and Scalabrini 2021).

References

Berberian N, Fogel S, Northoff G (2022) Neural synchrony mediates dreams. In preparation.

Blanke O, Slater M, Serino A (2015) Behavioral, neural, and computational principles of bodily self-consciousness. Neuron. Oct 7;88(1):145–166. doi: 10.1016/j.neuron.2015.09.029

Christoff K, Irving ZC, Fox KC, Spreng RN, Andrews-Hanna JR (2016) Mind-wandering as spontaneous thought: A dynamic framework. Nat Rev Neurosci. Nov;17(11):718–731. doi: 10.1038/nrn.2016.113. Epub 2016 Sep 22.

Conio B, Martino M, Magioncalda P, Escelsior A, Inglese M, Amore M, Northoff G (2020) Opposite effects of dopamine and serotonin on resting-state networks: Review and implications for psychiatric disorders. Mol Psychiatry. Jan;25(1):82–93. doi: 10.1038/s41380-019-0406-4. Epub 2019 Apr 5.

Domhoff GW, Fox KC (2015) Dreaming and the default network: A review, synthesis, and counterintuitive research proposal. Conscious Cogn. May;33:342–353. doi: 10.1016/j.concog.2015.01.019. Epub 2015 Feb 24.

Fogel SM, Ray LB, Sergeeva V, De Koninck J, Owen AM (2018) A novel approach to dream content analysis reveals links between learning related dream incorporation and cognitive abilities. Front Psychol. Aug 6;9:1398. doi: 10.3389/fpsyg.2018.01398. eCollection 2018.

Fox KC, Dixon ML, Nijeboer S, Girn M, Floman JL, Lifshitz M, Ellamil M, Sedlmeier P, Christoff K (2016) Functional neuroanatomy of meditation: A review and meta-analysis of 78 functional neuroimaging investigations. Neurosci Biobehav Rev. Jun;65:208–228. doi: 10.1016/j.neubiorev.2016.03.021. Epub 2016 Mar 28.

Fox KC, Nijeboer S, Solomonova E, Domhoff GW, Christoff K (2013) Dreaming as mind wandering: Evidence from functional neuroimaging and first-person content reports. Front Hum Neuroscience. Jul 30;7:412. doi: 10.3389/fnhum.2013.00412. eCollection 2013.

Golesorkhi M, Gomez-Pilar J, Tumati S, Fraser M, Northoff G (2021a) Temporal hierarchy of intrinsic neural timescales converges with spatial core-periphery organization. Commun Biol. Mar 4;4(1):277. doi: 10.1038/s42003-021-01785-z

Golesorkhi M, Gomez-Pilar J, Zilio F, Berberian N, Wolff A, Yagoub MCE, Northoff G (2021b) The brain and its time: Intrinsic neural timescales are key for input processing. Commun Biol. Aug 16;4(1):970. doi: 10.1038/s42003-021-02483-6

Hobson JA (2009) REM sleep and dreaming: Towards a theory of proto-consciousness. Nat Rev Neurosci. Nov;10(11):803–813. doi: 10.1038/nrn2716. Epub 2009 Oct 1. PMID: 19794431 Review.

Hua J, Zhang Y, Wolff A, Northoff G (2021) Thought dynamics is mediated by alpha and theta peak frequency. Nature Communication Biology. in press.

Huang Z, Obara N, Davis HH 4th, Pokorny J, Northoff G (2016) The temporal structure of resting-state brain activity in the medial prefrontal cortex predicts self-consciousness. Neuropsychologia. Feb;82:161–170. doi: 10.1016/j.neuropsychologia.2016.01.025. Epub 2016 Jan 21.

Kolvoort IR, Wainio-Theberge S, Wolff A, Northoff G (2020) Temporal integration as "common currency" of brain and self-scale-free activity in resting-state EEG correlates with temporal delay effects on self-relatedness. Hum Brain Mapp. Oct 15;41(15):4355–4374. doi: 10.1002/hbm.25129. Epub 2020 Jul 22.

Leuzinger-Bohleber M, et al (2019) Dreams. In: Neuropsychodynamic psychiatry, ed. H Boeker, P Hartwich, G Northoff. Springer, New York, Heidelberg.

Lin YS, Hartwich P, Wolff A, Golesorkhi M, Northoff G (2020) The self in art therapy: Brain-based assessment of the drawing process. Med Hypotheses. May;138:109596. doi: 10.1016/j.mehy.2020.109596. Epub 2020 Jan 23.

Martino M, Magioncalda P, Conio B, Capobianco L, Russo D, Adavastro G, Tumati S, Tan Z, Lee HC, Lane TJ, Amore M, Inglese M, Northoff G (2020) Abnormal functional relationship of sensorimotor network with neurotransmitter-related nuclei via subcortical-cortical loops in manic and depressive phases of bipolar disorder. Schizophr Bull. Jan 4;46(1):163–174. doi: 10.1093/schbul/sbz035

Northoff G (2011) Neuropsychoanalysis in practice. Oxford University Press, Oxford, New York.

Northoff G, Magioncalda P, Martino M, Lee HC, Tseng YC, Lane T (2018) Too fast or too slow? Time and neuronal variability in bipolar disorder- A combined theoretical and empirical investigation. Schizophr Bull. Jan 13;44(1):54–64. doi: 10.1093/schbul/sbx050

Northoff G, Qin P (2011) How can the brain's resting state activity generate hallucinations? A 'resting state hypothesis' of auditory verbal hallucinations. Schizophr Res. Apr;127(1–3):202–214. doi: 10.1016/j.schres.2010.11.009. Epub 2010 Dec 13.

Northoff G, Scalabrini A (2021) "Project for a spatiotemporal neuroscience": Brain and psyche share their topography and dynamic. Front Psychol. Oct 14;12:717402. doi: 10.3389/fpsyg.2021.717402. eCollection 2021.

Northoff G, Wainio-Theberge S, Evers K (2020a) Is temporo-spatial dynamics the "common currency" of brain and mind? In quest of "spatiotemporal neuroscience". Phys Life Rev. Jul;33:34–54. doi: 10.1016/j.plrev.2019.05.002. Epub 2019 May 23.

Northoff G, Wainio-Theberge S, Evers K (2020b) Spatiotemporal neuroscience: What is it and why we need it. Phys Life Rev. Jul;33:78–87. doi: 10.1016/j.plrev.2020.06.005. Epub 2020 Jul 10.

Panksepp J, Biven L (2012) The archaeology of mind. Norton Publisher, New York.

Qin P, Wang M, Northoff G (2020) Linking bodily, environmental and mental states in the self-A three-level model based on a meta-analysis. Neurosci Biobehav Rev. Aug;115:77–95. doi: 10.1016/j.neubiorev.2020.05.004. Epub 2020 May 31.

Qin P, Wu X, Wu C, Wu H, Zhang J, Huang Z, Weng X, Zang D, Qi Z, Tang W, Hiromi T, Tan J, Tanabe S, Fogel S, Hudetz AG, Yang Y, Stamatakis EA, Mao Y, Northoff G (2021) Higher-order sensorimotor circuit of the brain's global network supports human consciousness. Neuroimage. May 1;231:117850. doi: 10.1016/j.neuroimage.2021.117850. Epub 2021 Feb 12.

Solms M (2015) The feeling brain. Routledge, London, New York.

Solms M (2020) Project for a (new) psychology. Neuropsychoanalysis. 23–45.

Solms M (2021) The hidden spring: A journey to the source of consciousness. Norton Publisher, New York.

Spagnoli R, Northoff G (2021) The dynamic self. Routledge Publisher, London, New York.

Tanabe S, Huang Z, Zhang J, Chen Y, Fogel S, Doyon J, Wu J, Xu J, Zhang J, Qin P, Wu X, Mao Y, Mashour GA, Hudetz AG, Northoff G (2020) Altered global brain signal during physiologic, pharmacologic, and pathologic states of unconsciousness in humans and rats. Anesthesiology. Jun;132(6):1392–1406. doi: 10.1097/ALN.0000000000003197

Vanhaudenhuyse A, Demertzi A, Schabus M, Noirhomme Q, Bredart S, Boly M, Phillips C, Soddu A, Luxen A, Moonen G, Laureys SJ (2011) Two distinct neuronal networks mediate the awareness of environment and of self. Cogn Neurosci. Mar;23(3):570–578. doi: 10.1162/jocn.2010.21488. Epub 2010 Jun 1.

Windt JM (2010) The immersive spatiotemporal hallucination model of dreaming. Phenomenol Cogn Sci. 9(2):295–316.

Windt JM (2021) How deep is the rift between conscious states in sleep and wakefulness? Spontaneous experience over the sleep-wake cycle. Philos Trans R Soc Lond B Biol Sci. Feb;376(1817):20190696. doi: 10.1098/rstb.2019.0696. Epub 2020 Dec 14.

Windt JM, Noreika V (2011) How to integrate dreaming into a general theory of consciousness–A critical review of existing positions and suggestions for future research. Conscious Cogn. Dec;20(4):1091–1107. doi: 10.1016/j.concog.2010.09.010. Epub 2010 Oct 8. PMID: 20933438 Review.

Wolff A, Di Giovanni DA, Gómez-Pilar J, Nakao T, Huang Z, Longtin A, Northoff G (2019) The temporal signature of self: Temporal measures of resting-state EEG predict self-consciousness. Hum Brain Mapp. Feb 15;40(3):789–803. doi: 10.1002/hbm.24412. Epub 2018 Oct 4.

Zhang J, Huang Z, Tumati S, Northoff G (2020) Rest-task modulation of fMRI-derived global signal topography is mediated by transient coactivation patterns. PLoS Biol. Jul 10;18(7):e3000733. doi: 10.1371/journal.pbio.3000733. eCollection 2020 Jul.

Zhang J, Northoff G (2021) Function of the global signal: Dual layer model. Neuroimage, in press.

Zilio F, Gomez-Pilar J, Cao S, Zhang J, Zang D, Qi Z, Tan J, Hiromi T, Wu X, Fogel S, Huang Z, Hohmann MR, Fomina T, Synofzik M, Grosse-Wentrup M, Owen AM, Northoff G (2021) Are intrinsic neural timescales related to sensory processing? Evidence from abnormal behavioral states. Neuroimage. Feb 1;226:117579. doi: 10.1016/j.neuroimage.2020.117579. Epub 2020 Nov 20.

Chapter 7

Schizophrenia and depression

Introduction

We already showed that the self operates on a continuum between
healthy and pathological states, as in narcissism, trauma, and dissociation. This leaves open the very extreme pathological end
of that continuum where psychiatric disorders like schizophrenia
and major depressive disorders (in the following simply termed
depression) are "located". We show how the spatiotemporal
approach can yield novel insight into the neuronal mechanisms
of the typical psychodynamic features like introjection in depression and projection in schizophrenia.

We will discuss topographic and dynamic changes in the
brain's neural activity in schizophrenia and depression. That,
in turn, serves as stepping stone for understanding the psychodynamic changes in these disorders. Given the constraints of
this book, I cannot focus on all the psychodynamic or neuronal
details in depression and schizophrenia. For that, I refer to specific papers and books (Boeker et al. 2019). I therefore focus on
some psychodynamic core features. Introjection is a typical characteristic of depression, while increased projection is a psychodynamic hallmark feature of schizophrenia. This lets me focus
on object relations as well as how objects are related to the self
in these disorders.

DOI: 10.4324/9781003132905-8

Part I: schizophrenia and projection

Topography of schizophrenia I – reverse representation of global brain activity

We already encountered the brain's global activity and how it is locally represented in specific regions (see Chapter 4). Roughly, the brain exhibits global activity that can be measured by the global signal in fMRI. Additionally, the GS is represented in the activity levels of different regions in distinct degrees, thus showing a certain spatial topography. For instance, GS in healthy subjects is more strongly represented in the lower-order sensory and motor regions, that is, input and output regions, than in higher-order more cognitive association regions like the prefrontal cortex and the DMN (Wang et al. 2019; Yang et al. 2017; Zhang et al. 2020).

This is no longer the case in schizophrenia. Here the spatial topography of GS is different, if not reversed. The brain's global activity is no longer represented most strongly within the lower-order sensory input and motor output regions like the sensory and motor cortices. Instead, it is now more strongly represented within the higher-order association cortices like the prefrontal and parietal cortex and DMN (Yang et al. 2017; Wang et al. 2019). The local–regional re-redistribution of GS is especially related to positive symptoms like delusion and hallucination: the more strongly the global brain activity is re-distributed from lower-order sensori-motor to higher-order association cortices, the more severe the symptoms, like hallucinations and delusions

Together, these findings show that lower-order sensori-motor systems that process external inputs (and outputs) stand in an abnormal if not reverse relationship to those higher-order associative regions that process internally oriented contents, that is, higher-order neural systems. The boundaries between internally and externally oriented cognition are consequently blurred, leading to what psychodynamically is described as the "blurring of the inner ego boundaries" (Federn 1952): the boundaries of the internal self (including its self-objects, as pointed out by Kohut) can no longer be properly distinguished from the objects of the external environment.

Topography of schizophrenia II – reduced rest/ prestimulus – task modulation

Given the reverse topography of lower- and higher-order regions in schizophrenia, one would suspect that internally oriented cognition including the self interacts in an abnormal if not reduced way with external objects or events. For that, we need to take into view the interaction of resting state/prestimulus and task-related activity. How can we characterize such rest/prestimulus-task interaction? Internally oriented cognition already takes place during the spontaneous activity as measured in resting state and prestimulus activity, while external objects or events induce what is described as task-related activity. Since task-related activity is preceded by prestimulus activity, which mirrors the brain's spontaneous activity, we need to consider how the latter interacts with and modulates the former.

The blurring of internally and externally oriented cognition in schizophrenia should be related to lower differentiation of resting state/prestimulus and task-related activity. This was investigated in a recent study by Northoff and Gomez-Pillar (2021). They first conducted a meta-analysis of all EEG and fMRI studies in schizophrenia, including both resting state/prestimulus activity and task-related activity. They observe that, relative to prestimulus or resting state activity, task-related activity in different tasks was significantly reduced in schizophrenia: they were no longer able to properly differentiate their task-related activity from the ongoing prestimulus or resting state activity.

This, in a second step, was complemented by our own EEG studies showing that the altered (enhanced or reduced depending on the measure) prestimulus connectivity between regions made it impossible for the external stimulus (an auditory tone) to increase activity level. Task-related activity could thus no longer be properly differentiated from the prestimulus activity: this entails that the external contents, that is, the auditory tone, could no longer be properly distinguished from the ongoing internally oriented cognition including the self.

Psychodynamic of schizophrenia I – confusion of internally and externally oriented cognition

What are the mechanisms through which resting state changes and/ or reduced rest/prestimulus-task modulation impact cognition and especially its differentiation of internally and externally oriented cognition? Predictive coding could be one such mechanism, since it modulates the contents of both internally and externally oriented cognition. Roughly, predictive coding assumes that the predicted input or empirical prior, which is based on the prestimulus or resting state dynamic, strongly shapes subsequent task-related activity, with the latter being the manifestation of the prediction error, that is, the comparison of predicted and actual input. Given their altered input processing, schizophrenia subjects may suffer from a high prediction error – they are often wrong in their predictions about the external environment (and ultimately also being wrong about their own internal self).

It is well known that especially the generation of the predicted input is abnormal in schizophrenia; this is distributed and reverberates across the whole brain and its cortical hierarchy, affecting basically all cognitive and psychological domains. These abnormalities in the predicted input or empirical prior during rest or prestimulus period impact the internal contents of internally oriented cognition, including self-referential processing, mind wandering, and mental time travel, with changes in these being well recorded in schizophrenia.

At the same time, the abnormal prestimulus dynamics may, through its extreme degrees, lose the ability or capacity to change during the external stimuli, that is, the subsequent task states of the brain that are elicited by the external contents of externally oriented cognition. The resulting prediction error may consequently be abnormally high, as it is more strongly determined by the predicted input, that is, the internal content of the own self, than the external content of the environment – internal contents (i.e., self and self-objects in psychodynamic terms) dominate even during externally oriented perception and cognition (i.e., objects in psychodynamic terms).

Psychodynamic of schizophrenia II – reduced differentiation of self/self-objects and objects

Given the topographic changes and reduced rest/prestimulus-task modulation, the transient external stimuli or tasks are perceived and cognized in abnormal proximity to the internal contents of the own self (and its self-objects). Ultimately, this leads to the confusion of internally and externally oriented cognition contents: the different origins or sources of the different cognition contents, that is, internal self and external environment, can no longer be distinguished and monitored by the subjects, that is, source monitoring deficits (Nelson et al. 2020; Sass et al. 2018).

Psychodynamically, the confusion of self and object as well as of self-objects and objects has been highlighted in schizophrenia (Northoff 2011; Boeker et al. 2019). Self and its self-objects are distinguished by contents that are generated internally by an internal source, that is, the own self, as manifested in internally oriented cognition, while what psychodynamically is described as object refers to the contents that have their ultimate source in the external world and are manifested in externally oriented cognition.

What neuronally is described in terms of rest/prestimulus-task interaction corresponds more or less to what psychologically is framed as interaction of internally and externally oriented cognition contents; the latter, in turn, may find its analogue in the psychodynamic distinction of self/self-object and object. Decreased self/self-object-object differentiation in schizophrenia may thus be traced to reduced separation of internally and externally oriented cognition, which, neuronally, may be based on reduced differentiation of task-related activity from the ongoing resting state/prestimulus activity. We can thus yield a neuropsychodynmaic hypothesis where increased projection of the own internal self onto external objects in schizophrenia is related to decreased rest/prestimulus-task interaction.

Dynamic of schizophrenia I – reduced alignment and entrainment

Why and how are schizophrenia subjects so disconnected from their respective environmental context? In a seminal study, Lakatos (Lakatos et al. 2013) conducted an EEG study in schizophrenic patients to whom they presented a stream of auditory stimuli (i.e., tones) with regular, that is, rhythmic interstimulus intervals (1500 ms). They presented the stream of auditory stimuli with some deviant stimuli (20%) that were distinguished in their frequency. Subjects had to either passively listen (passive task), detect the easily detectable deviant stimuli (easy task), or detect the more difficult (variation by frequency) detectable stimuli (difficult task).

The authors measured what is called phase coherence (i.e., intertrial coherence; ITC) that refers to the synchronization of the brain's phase fluctuations with the timing of the external stimuli. As expected, increased task difficulty lead to higher ITC (in 1–4 Hz/delta) in healthy subjects. In contrast, such a task-related increase in delta ITC was not observed in schizophrenic patients. These patients were thus not able to properly align, or shift, their auditory cortical phase onsets in the delta range (that corresponded to the stimulation frequency of the presented tones) to the onset of the external tones – they could not adapt their internal neural activity to the external task. This suggests decreased phase alignment or entrainment to external auditory stimuli.

Finally, reduced delta ITC correlated with both the behavioral measure, such as the detection rate of the deviant tones, and the electrophysiological index, the P300 (in response to deviant tones), in schizophrenic subjects. Importantly, reduced delta ITC also predicted the severity of psychopathological symptoms (as measured with the Brief Psychiatric Rating Scale/BPRS) and especially the positive symptoms (that include hallucinations, delusions, and excitement) (Lakatos et al. 2013).

Abnormal, that is, reduced, entrainment of phase onsets to external stimuli has also been observed in other studies in schizophrenia, such as in response to 40-hz auditory stimuli (Hamm et al. 2015; Hamm et al. 2011). Other studies also observed major abnormalities in phase resetting in delta (1–4 Hz) and theta (5–8 Hz) ranges in schizophrenia (Doege et al. 2010a; Doege et al. 2010b) during an auditory oddball task, which, even more interestingly, predicted the degree of positive symptoms in schizophrenia, such as disorganization (see also Hamm et al. 2011).

Taken together, these findings suggest that schizophrenic patients remain unable to properly link their internal auditory cortical neural activity, as indexed by phase onsets in delta, to a stream of external auditory stimuli. Lakatos et al. (2013) speak of deficits in active predictive sensing by phase resetting that does not allow schizophrenic patients to increase their cortical excitability at stimulus onset for the subsequent processing of external stimuli. Hence, the deficit in input synchronization, as one may say, impacts the subject's capacity to predict subsequent stimuli, including their timing and content.

Dynamic of schizophrenia II – deficit in the timing with temporal discoordination

Where and how is such a deficit in phase synchronization with external stimuli coming from? Wolff et al. (2022) investigated schizophrenia in an auditory task (oddball). She again, like Lakatos and others, observed deficits in the ITC, as schizophrenia participants could not synchronize their brain's phase onset to the onsets of the external stimuli. In a second step, Wolff et al. (2022) investigated temporal coordination of ITC. Given that all subjects were exposed to the same stimuli at the same time, she correlated the subjects' neural activity among or between the subjects. As expected, this yielded high inter-subjective ITC correlation among the healthy subjects.

In contrast, there was no such inter-subjective ITC correlation among the schizophrenia subjects, nor of the schizophrenia subjects with the healthy subjects. Providing further simulation and modeling, Wolff et al. (2022) conclude that neural activity in schizophrenia may exhibit abnormal temporal discoordination, which, in turn, deteriorates their ability to phase synchronize with external stimuli. This, as Wolff et al. (2022) also showed, renders the schizophrenia brain too noisy, with decreased signal-to-noise ratio (SNR) during the processing of external inputs.

Taken together, these results strongly suggest that schizophrenia subjects are no longer able to temporally synchronize their internal neural activity with the external activity in the environment. This means that their brain can no longer process the external inputs from the world properly – which speaks to a basic temporal deficit in input processing in schizophrenia. Schizophrenia subjects and their brains are thus neuronally decoupled from the environment – such "decoupling from the environment" has been described phenomenologically as "loss of vital contact with reality" (Minkowski 1927), or "crisis of common sense" (Stanghellini 2000).

Dynamic of schizophrenia III – reduced temporal integration of inputs

Complementing EEG, input processing has also been probed in a recent fMRI study by Wengler et al. (2020). Inputs are mediated through sensory systems like the visual, auditory, and somatosensory systems. Wengler et al. (2020) traced the different regions from bottommost to topmost in these three input stream systems by measuring their intrinsic neural timescales, that is, their autocorrelation window. They observed that healthy subjects exhibited a continuous increase, that is, longer duration in ACW from bottom to top, within each of the three input processing streams.

Longer duration in ACW means that from bottom to top, more and more external stimuli occurring at distinct time points can be integrated with each other – this yields complex perceptual and cognitive contents (Himberger et al. 2018). Schizophrenia participants, in contrast, no longer showed such a hierarchy of ACW with bottom-to-top progression within each of the three input processing streams. This means that they, unlike healthy subjects, can no longer properly integrate different external inputs and thus cannot constitute complex perceptual and cognitive contents; instead, perceptual and cognitive contents are fragmented due to lack of temporal integration which dominate their time experience (Fuchs and Van Duppen 2017; Arantes-Gonçalves et al. 2021).

The schizophrenic subjects can consequently no longer perceive any difference between different events in the external environment nor a difference of the latter to their own ongoing internal mental or cognitive events, that is, their self. They subsequently confuse their internal self with the external environment (and vice versa), as is typical in symptoms like auditory hallucination, delusions, thought disorder, and ego and passivity disturbances.

Psychodynamic of schizophrenia III – loss of object relation and projection

Together, the neuroscientific findings show decreases in different temporal features of external input processing, including input entrainment and input differentiation. Importantly, these findings point to a temporal deficit in the neural activity during external input processing: neural activity is no longer temporally organized in a coherent and coordinated way, which makes it impossible to phase synchronize to and temporally integrate external inputs (Wolff et al. 2021). As a consequence, neural activity related to external (and ultimately also internal) inputs is temporally fragmented – this is manifest psychologically in the experience of temporal fragmentation (Stanghellini et al. 2016; Fuchs 2019).

The loss of input processing is related to what psychodynamically is described as the "loss of object relation" as based on decreased investment of energy (cathexis), that is, "decathexis of objects" (Boeker et al. 2019; Northoff 2011). This has already been pointed out by Freud himself in his famous case of Schreber: "The patient has withdrawn from the people in his environment and form the external world generally the libidinal cathexis which he has hitherto directed onto them. Thus everything has become indifferent and irrelevant to him" (Freud 1911, 74) (see also Hartwich and Northoff in Boeker et al. 2019, 184ff, for different notions of cathexis in schizophrenia).

The loss of object relation carries major psychopathological implications. If one can no longer perceive externally oriented contents in a synchronized and integrated way, one's perception turns inwards to internally oriented contents like delusions and hallucinations: these are the internal substitutes of the missing external perceptual contents the schizophrenic patients assume to be out there in the external world – they are internal "paraconstructions" of a lost external world (Hartwich and Northoff in Boeker et al. 2019, 184ff). "Para-constructions" can be viewed as redirection of the cathexis from the external to the internal objects – this is manifest in increased projection of one's own internal self/self-objects to the external environment as in hallucination and delusion.

Part II: depression and introjection

Topography of depression I – disbalance between medial and lateral prefrontal cortex

Major depressive disorder, abbreviated as depression in the following, shows major topographic changes in the brain. In a meta-analysis combining human and animal data, Alcaro (Alcaro et al. 2010) looked at the brain's resting state activity, that is, the neural activity that can be observed in different regions and networks during the absence of specific stimuli or tasks. This yielded hyperactive regions in the medial prefrontal cortex like the perigenual anterior cingulate cortex (PACC) and ventromedial prefrontal cortex (VMPFC) (as well as subcortical midline regions such as thalamic regions like the dorsomedial thalamus and the pulvinar and pallidum/putamen and midbrain regions like the ventral tegmental area [VTA], substantia nigra [SN], tectum, and periaqueductal gray [PAG]).

In contrast, resting-state activity was hypoactive in the lateral prefrontal cortex regions, being reduced in the dorsolateral prefrontal cortex (DLPFC) (and other regions like the posterior cingulate cortex [PCC] and adjacent precuneus/cuneus; Alcaro et al. 2010) (see also Kaiser et al. 2015 for similar results). Especially the medial prefrontal resting state hyperactivity changes in PACC and VMPFC seem to be somehow specific for depression, as they are not observed in other psychiatric disorders (see Kaiser et al 2015).

The medial prefrontal regions like the PACC and VMPFC are core regions of the default-mode network, while lateral prefrontal regions like the DLPFC a part of the central executive network. A meta-analysis of resting state functional connectivity observed the following abnormal changes in these networks that seem to be (more or less) specific to MDD as distinguished from other psychiatric disorders (Kaiser et al. 2015). The DMN shows functional hyperconnectivity among its regions, especially between the anterior and posterior midline regions. In contrast to the regions within the DMN, regions within the CEN show functional hypoconnectivity and are also less connected to parietal regions implicated in attention towards the external environment.

This suggests spatial disbalance between the two networks, with an abnormal spatial shift towards the DMN and away from the CEN, with the former also enslaving the latter (as suggested by abnormally negative functional hyperconnectivity between DMN and CEN; Kaiser et al. 2015). These findings are specific to MDD, as in bipolar disorder (BD), such a pattern cannot be observed (Martino et al. 2016) while in schizophrenia, functional connectivity between the DMN and CEN is positive (rather than abnormally negative, as in MDD) (Carthart-Harris et al. 2013).

Topography of depression II – increased self-focus and decreased environment-focus

The data provide evidence for abnormal resting state hyperactivity in medial prefrontal regions as part of the DMN in MDD, while there is resting state hypoactivity in lateral prefrontal regions as part of the CEN. This suggests the opposite, that is, reciprocal modulation between the medial and lateral prefrontal cortex, with resting state activity being abnormally increased in the former and decreased in the latter.

Abnormal opposite or reciprocal modulation between medial and lateral prefrontal cortical resting state activity in MDD is further supported by analogous functional connectivity: increased functional connectivity in PACC-VMPFC and thus within DMN is accompanied by decreased functional connectivity in the lateral prefrontal cortex and the CEN (Hasler and Northoff 2011; Northoff 2014a; Northoff and Synille 2014). One can thus speak of abnormal reciprocal modulation between the medial/DMN and lateral/CEN prefrontal cortex, with their spatial balance tilting abnormally towards the former at the expense of the latter.

How now is the abnormal spatial balance between the medial and lateral prefrontal cortex related to the psychopathological symptoms in MDD? This spatial imbalance on the level of the brain's spontaneous activity is well reflected on the phenomenal level: MDD patients' experiences are characterized by an increased focus on their own internal contents as consisting in either thoughts, as in ruminations with "increased self-focus", and/or the body, leading to various unspecific somatic symptoms, such as "increased body-focus" (Northoff 2016a, 2016b).

In contrast, these patients' experience is no longer focused on the external environment at all, for example, "decreased environment-focus", which psychopathologically is manifest in social withdrawal and lack of motivation. One can consequently say that the abnormal spatial structure in the brain's spontaneous activity translates and surfaces in the spatial structure of experience, that is, the spatial organization of contents with regard to body, self, and environment, which in turn leads to the various kinds of psychopathological symptoms.

Topography of depression III – DMN "enslaves and magnetizes" the rest of the brain

Why and how is there such abnormal neuronal disbalance? For that, Andrea Scalabrini, a very gifted Italian neuroscientist and psychoanalyst, investigated fMRI-based global brain activity and its local–regional representation in major depressive disorder (Scalabrini et al. 2020). Global brain activity can be measured by the functional connectivity between all regions of the brain – the average of all their connections is the global signal. One then correlates GS with the time series of each region, that is, global signal correlation (GSCORR), which gives us the degree to which the former is represented in the different regions of the brain, that is, GS topography.

What did Andrea Scalabrini find? He observed that the brain's global activity is much more strongly represented in the regions of the default-mode network in depression compared to healthy subjects. In short, the DMN concentrates the brain's global activity on itself.

How about the connections of the DMN to the rest of the brain, the non-DMN like the various lower-order sensory regions like visual and auditory networks? For that, he investigated the functional connectivity of the DMN to all non-DMN regions. Most interestingly, he observed that all non-DMN networks were too strongly connected with the DMN in depression: the DMN "enslaves" and "magnetizes" the non-DMN, that is, the rest of the brain, hence the title of Scalabrini's paper, "All Roads Lead to the DMN" (Scalabrini et al. 2020). Finally, the researchers could also show that, using machine learning, the degree to which global brain activity focused on the DMN and enslaved its connection to the non-DMN highly predicted whether the subjects were healthy or depressed (more than 90% accuracy of prediction). This suggests that the global DMN–non-DMN topography may represent a basic disturbance that underlies and drives depression.

Psychodynamic of depression I – increased introjection

Together, MDD can be characterized by a too-strong DMN relative to the rest of the brain, that is, non-DMN. This means that the DMN "enslaves" the rest of the brain; it, according to Andrea Scalabrini, operates as a "too strong magnet" for the non-DMN. This means that the signals and stimuli processed in the non-DMN are abnormally strongly impacted by the DMN. On the psychological level, this means that everything is perceived in terms of the DMN and its self – the brain's global focus is on the DMN, which psychologically is mirrored in an analogous global psychological focus on the self, the "increased self-focus" (Northoff 2016a, 2016b). This happens mainly on the mental or cognitive layer of the self, as that is based on the DMN (see Chapter 1). However, that may also affect the lower layers of the self, like its extero-proprioceptive and interoceptive layers, as manifest in the often rather strong somatic bodily symptoms of depression.

In contrast, the environmental inputs as mainly processed in the lower-order non-DMN regions are not as functionally highlighted by the brain's global brain topography – the brain's global focus on the processing of external inputs from the environment is reduced, resulting psychologically in "decreased environment-focus". We can thus see that the brain's neuronal topography of increased DMN vs decreased non-DMN is well mirrored by an almost analogous mental or psychic topography of increased self-focus vs decreased environment-focus. Hence, neuronal topography transforms into psychic topography. The topographical spatial disbalance thus provides the shared feature, that is, "common currency", of brain and psyche in depression.

Psychodynamically, the DMN-based increased self-focus corresponds well to what is described as introjection. Depressed subjects introject external content by abnormally strongly relating them to their own self: this may be traced to the function of the DMN and its self operating as an abnormally strong magnet that attracts, enslaves, and magnetizes all non-self-specific contents, as Andrea Scalabrini says. Increased introjection thus goes along with loss of actual object relations and, even more importantly, abnormally strong reactualization of the lost object (self-object, if one follows Kohut).

Dynamic of depression – input processing is too slow and reduced

Objects are typically about external events in the environment. To better understand changes in object relation in depression, we must investigate how the brain's input processing is affected in depression. To investigate input processing in depression, we focus on the visual or occipital cortex (OC) as a paradigmatic example. OC processes visual input, and it is well known that depressed subjects perceive their environment in mainly gray, static, and coarse-grained ways (Song et al. 2021; Fitzgerald 2013). Additionally, depressed subjects perceive their own inner time speed as too slow (Fuchs 2019; Northoff et al. 2018). Together, these psychological observations raise the question of whether neural activity in OC is too slow. This was investigated in two recent papers of ours by Song et al. (2021, 2022).

We first observed that OC neural activity is indeed not fast enough; that is, it is too slow. In fMRI we could observe decreased representation of global brain activity in specifically the faster frequencies (slow 3: 0.073 to 0.198 Hz) of the signal (Song et al. 2022). Analogous findings were obtained in the faster frequency range (1–50 Hz) of EEG. Here again, OC activity was too slow as measured by median frequency (MF) and autocorrelation window. Moreover, the abnormally slow activity in the OC resting state impacted its responsiveness to external inputs during task-related activity: the latter was simply too slow in depression to process especially fast inputs.

Most interestingly, the too-slow OC activity was abnormally strongly connected with the cortical midline regions of the DMN. This, again, was observed in both fMRI and EEG. Accordingly, the enslavement of OC by DMN, that is, their increased functional connectivity, is related to decreased speed in the temporal dynamics of OC itself, that is, too-slow neural activity.

Finally, Song et al. (2021, 2022) tested whether abnormally slow OC activity affects visual perception in an analogous way with the perception being too slow. They indeed could show that depressed subjects showed deficits in visual perception, that is, motion surround suppression, during specifically faster visual stimuli, whereas no such deficit was observed during slower stimuli. That suggests that the abnormal slowness is manifested on both neuronal and psychological-perceptual levels – it provides the "common currency" of brain and psyche.

Psychodynamic of depression II – reduced actual objects and identification with the lost object

What do these findings tell us for the psychodynamic of depression? If the input processing is too slow, some of the respectively associated contents may get lost – the brain is simply too slow or sluggish to process all of the usually fast incoming inputs as related to the actual objects of the external environment. The person can no longer associate and relate the external objects to its own self – this results in what psychodynamically is described as "loss of actual object relation" (Northoff 2011; Boeker et al. 2019).

If there are no actual external objects processed anymore related to the own self, the balance of actual-external vs past-internal objects shifts towards the latter. Typically, depressed subjects refer to past objects of their internal memories (like self-objects, to use Kohutian terms) that are lost, like the lost mother or father. All energy, that is, their cathexis, is invested in those lost objects – the latter are thereby reactivated and identified with the own self in the mental life of the depressed subjects.

Freud describes this very vividly in terms of the libido:

> But the libido was not displaced onto another object, it was withdrawn into the ego. There, however, it was not employed in an unspecific way, but served to establish an identification of the ego with abandoned object. Thus the shadow of the object fell upon the ego, and the latter could henceforth be judged by a special agency, as though it were an object, the forsaken object. In this way, an object-loss was transformed into an ego-loss and the conflict between the ego and the loved person into a cleavage between the critical activity of the ego and the ego as altered by identification.
>
> (p. 299)

The abnormal focus on the ego or self may neuronally be based upon the abnormally strong representation of the DMN in the brain's global activity – the DMN and its internal self magnetize and slow down the input processing of the actual external objects, for instance, in the OC. The actual objects are then replaced by increased focus on the past and its lost objects: if no actual external objects are processed, one needs to revert to the more internal objects of the past, including the lost ones, to stabilize the self (through internal rather than external self-objects). This, in turn, initiates the abnormal identification of the ego or self with the lost object Freud describes so well. Accordingly, the combination of increased global DMN representation and abnormally slow non-DMN or sensory like OC input processing may lead to the strange combination of decreased actual external object relation and increased reactivation of past and lost internal objects.

Conclusion

Can neuropsychoanalysis contribute to a better understanding of the most extreme changes of our psyche in psychiatric disorders like schizophrenia and depression? Though not the main focus of psychoanalysis, I consider the explanation of these psychiatric disorders a "litmus test" for neuropsychoanalysis. Only if neuropsychoanalysis can properly account for these psychiatric disorders, namely their self-disturbances, symptoms, and psychodynamic mechanisms, may it provide a proper model of brain and psyche.

Recent neuroscientific findings about the brain's abnormal spatial topography and its temporal dynamics can provide novel insights into the abnormal psychodynamic mechanisms like object relation, ego/self, introjection and projection, paraconstruction, and self–self-object/object relation in schizophrenia and depression. The explanatory power of neuropsychoanalysis for these psychiatric disorders strongly supports the view that spatial topography and temporal dynamic do indeed serve as "common currency" of brain and psyche (Northoff et al. 2020a, 2020b; Northoff and Scalabrini 2021). Even more importantly, such a spatiotemporal topographic-dynamic view may prove fruitful clinically for developing a novel psychopathology, "spatiotemporal psychopathology" (Northoff 2016a, 2016b), as proper ground for more efficient and objective diagnosis and therapy of these psychiatric disorders.

References

Alcaro A, Panksepp J, Witczak J, Hayes DJ, Northoff G (2010) Is subcortical-cortical midline activity in depression mediated by glutamate and GABA? A cross-species translational approach. Neurosci Biobehav Reviews. Mar;34(4):592–605. doi: 10.1016/j.neubiorev.2009.11.023. Epub 2009 Dec 1. PMID: 19958790 Review.

Arantes-Gonçalves F, Wolman A, Bastos-Leite AJ, Northoff G (2021) Scale for space and time experience in psychosis: Converging phenomenological and psychopathological perspectives. Psychopathology. Dec 6:1–11. doi: 10.1159/000519500. Online ahead of print.

Boeker H, Hartwich P, Northoff G (Eds) (2019) Neuropsychodynamic psychiatry. Springer, Heidelberg, New York.

Carhart-Harris RL, Leech R, Erritzoe D, Williams TM, Stone JM, Evans J, Sharp DJ, Feilding A, Wise RG, Nutt DJ (2013) Functional connectivity measures after psilocybin inform a novel hypothesis of early psychosis. Schizophr Bull. Nov;39(6):1343–1351. doi: 10.1093/schbul/sbs117. Epub 2012 Oct 8.

Doege K, Jansen M, Mallikarjun P, Liddle EB, Liddle PF (2010a) How much does phase resetting contribute to event-related EEG abnormalities in schizophrenia? Neurosci Lett. Aug 30;481(1):1–5. doi: 10.1016/j.neulet.2010.06.008. Epub 2010 Jun 16.

Doege K, Kumar M, Bates AT, Das D, Boks MP, Liddle PF (2010b) Time and frequency domain event-related electrical activity associated with response control in schizophrenia. Clin Neurophysiol. Oct;121(10):1760–1771. doi: 10.1016/j.clinph.2010.03.049. Epub 2010 Apr 18.

Federn P (1952) Ego psychology and the psychoses. Basic Books, New York.

Fitzgerald PJ (2013) Gray colored glasses: Is major depression partially a sensory perceptual disorder? J Affect Disorders. Nov;151(2):418–422. doi: 10.1016/j.jad.2013.06.045. Epub 2013 Jul 29.

Freud S (1911) Psychoanalytic notes on an autobiographical account of a case of paranoia (Dementia Paranoides). Translated by Alix and James Strachey. Republished: 1979. Penguin Freud Library, London, New York.

Freud S (1917) Trauer und Melancholie (Mourning and melancholia). Internationale Zeitschrift für Ärztliche Psychoanalyse [International Journal for Medical Psychoanalysis]. 4(6):288–301.

Fuchs T, Stanghellini G (ed.) (2019) The experience of time and its disorders. In: The oxford handbook of phenomenological psychopathology (pp. 431–441). Oxford University Press, Oxford, New York.

Fuchs T, Van Duppen Z (2017) Time and events: On the phenomenology of temporal experience in schizophrenia (Ancillary article to EAWE domain 2). Psychopathology. 50(1):68–74. doi: 10.1159/000452768. Epub 2017 Jan 7.

Hamm JP, Bobilev AM, Hayrynen LK, Hudgens-Haney ME, Oliver WT, Parker DA, McDowell JE, Buckley PA, Clementz BA (2015) Stimulus train duration but not attention moderates gamma-band entrainment abnormalities in schizophrenia. Schizophr Res. Jun;165(1):97–102. doi: 10.1016/j.schres.2015.02.016. Epub 2015 Apr 11.

Hamm JP, Gilmore CS, Picchetti NA, Sponheim SR, Clementz BA (2011) Abnormalities of neuronal oscillations and temporal integration to low- and high-frequency auditory stimulation in schizophrenia. Biol Psychiatry. May 15;69(10):989–996. doi: 10.1016/j.biopsych.2010.11.021. Epub 2011 Jan 8.

Hasler G, Northoff G (2011) Discovering imaging endophenotypes for major depression. Mol Psychiatry. Jun;16(6):604–619. doi: 10.1038/mp.2011.23

Himberger KD, Chien HY, Honey CJ (2018) Principles of temporal processing across the cortical Hierarchy. Neuroscience. Oct 1;389:161–174. doi: 10.1016/j.neuroscience.2018.04.030. Epub 2018 May 2.

Kaiser RH, Andrews-Hanna JR, Wager TD, Pizzagalli DA (2015) Large-scale network dysfunction in major depressive disorder: A meta-analysis of resting-state functional connectivity. JAMA Psychiatry. Jun;72(6):603–611. doi: 10.1001/jamapsychiatry.2015.0071

Lakatos P, Schroeder CE, Leitman DI, Javitt DC (2013) Predictive suppression of cortical excitability and its deficit in schizophrenia. J Neurosci. Jul 10;33(28):11692–1702. doi: 10.1523/JNEUROSCI.0010-13.2013

Martino M, Magioncalda P, Huang Z, Conio B, Piaggio N, Duncan NW, Rocchi G, Escelsior A, Marozzi V, Wolff A, Inglese M, Amore M, Northoff G (2016) Contrasting variability patterns in the default mode and sensorimotor networks balance in bipolar depression and mania. Proc Natl Acad Sci U S A. Apr 26;113(17):4824–4829. doi: 10.1073/pnas.1517558113. Epub 2016 Apr 11.

Minkoswki E (1927) Lived time. Northwestern Press, Chicago.

Nelson B, Lavoie S, Gawęda Ł, Li E, Sass LA, Koren D, McGorry PD, Jack BN, Parnas J, Polari A, Allott K, Hartmann JA, Whitford TJ (2020) The neurophenomenology of early psychosis: An integrative empirical study. Conscious Cogn. Jan;77:102845. doi: 10.1016/j.concog.2019.102845. Epub 2019 Nov 1.

Northoff G (2011) Neuropsychoanalysis in practice. Oxford University Press, Oxford, New York.

Northoff G (2014a and b) Unlocking the brain, Vol I coding; Vol II consciousness. Oxford University Press, Oxford, New York.

Northoff G (2016a) Spatiotemporal psychopathology I: No rest for the brain's resting state activity in depression? Spatiotemporal psychopathology of depressive symptoms. J Affect Disord. Jan 15;190:854–866. doi: 10.1016/j.jad.2015.05.007. Epub 2015 May 14.

Northoff G (2016b) Spatiotemporal psychopathology II: How does a psychopathology of the brain's resting state look like? Spatiotemporal approach and the history of psychopathology. J Affect Disord. Jan 15;190:867–879. doi: 10.1016/j.jad.2015.05.008. Epub 2015 May 19.

Northoff G, Gomez-Pilar J (2021) Overcoming rest-task divide-abnormal temporospatial dynamics and its cognition in schizophrenia. Schizophr Bull. Apr 29;47(3):751–765. doi: 10.1093/schbul/sbaa178

Northoff G, Magioncalda P, Martino M, Lee HC, Tseng YC, Lane T (2018) Too fast or too slow? Time and neuronal variability in bipolar disorder- A combined theoretical and empirical investigation. Schizophr Bull. Jan 13;44(1):54–64. doi: 10.1093/schbul/sbx050

Northoff G, Scalabrini A (2021) "Project for a spatiotemporal neuroscience": Brain and psyche share their topography and dynamic. Front Psychol. Oct 14;12:717402. doi: 10.3389/fpsyg.2021.717402. eCollection 2021.

Northoff G, Sibille E (2014) Why are cortical GABA neurons relevant to internal focus in depression? A cross-level model linking cellular, biochemical and neural network findings. Mol Psychiatry. Sep;19(9):966–977. doi: 10.1038/mp.2014.68. Epub 2014 Jul 22.

Northoff G, Wainio-Theberge S, Evers K (2020a) Is temporo-spatial dynamics the "common currency" of brain and mind? In quest of "spatiotemporal neuroscience". Phys Life Rev. Jul;33:34–54. doi: 10.1016/j.plrev.2019.05.002. Epub 2019 May 23.

Northoff G, Wainio-Theberge S, Evers K (2020b) Spatiotemporal neuroscience: What is it and why we need it. Phys Life Rev. Jul;33:78–87. doi: 10.1016/j.plrev.2020.06.005. Epub 2020 Jul 10.

Sass L, Borda JP, Madeira L, Pienkos E, Nelson B (2018) Varieties of self disorder: A bio-pheno-social model of Schizophrenia. Schizophr Bull. Jun 6;44(4):720–727. doi: 10.1093/schbul/sby001

Scalabrini A, Vai B, Poletti S, Damiani S, Mucci C, Colombo C, Zanardi R, Benedetti F, Northoff G (2020) All roads lead to the default-mode network-global source of DMN abnormalities in major depressive disorder. Neuropsychopharmacology. Nov;45(12):2058–2069. doi: 10.1038/s41386-020-0785-x. Epub 2020.

Song XM, Hu XW, Li Z, Gao Y, Ju X, Liu DY, Wang QN, Xue C, Cai YC, Bai R, Tan ZL, Northoff G (2021) Reduction of higher-order occipital GABA and impaired visual perception in acute major depressive disorder. Mol Psychiatry. Apr 16. doi: 10.1038/s41380-021-01090-5. Online ahead of print.

Song XM, Hu XW, Li Z, Gao Y, Ju X, Liu DY, Wang QN, Xue C, Cai YC, Bai R, Tan ZL, Northoff G (2022) From neuronal to perceived speed in visual area MT. Submitted.

Stanghellini G (2000) Vulnerability to schizophrenia and lack of common sense. Schizophr Bull. 26(4):775–787. doi: 10.1093/oxfordjournals.schbul.a033493

Stanghellini G, Ballerini M, Presenza S, Mancini M, Raballo A, Blasi S, Cutting J (2016) Psychopathology of lived time: Abnormal time experience in persons with schizophrenia. Schizophr Bull. Jan;42(1):45–55. doi: 10.1093/schbul/sbv052. Epub 2015 May 4.

Wang X, Liao W, Han S, Li J, Zhang Y, Zhao J, Chen H (2019) Altered dynamic global signal topography in antipsychotic-naive adolescents with early-onset schizophrenia. Schizophr Res. 208:308–316.

Wengler K, Goldberg AT, Chahine G, Horga G (2020) Distinct hierarchical alterations of intrinsic neural timescales account for different manifestations of psychosis. Elife. Oct 27;9:e56151. doi: 10.7554/eLife.56151

Wolff A, Gomez-Pilar J, Zhang J, Choueiry J, de la Salle S, Knott V, Northoff G (2021) It's in the timing: Reduced temporal precision in neural activity of schizophrenia. Cereb Cortex. Dec 7:bhab425. doi: 10.1093/cercor/bhab425. Online ahead of print.

Yang GJ, Murray JD, Glasser M, Pearlson GD, Krystal JH, Schleifer C, Repovs G, Anticevic A (2017) Altered global signal topography in schizophrenia. Cereb Cortex. 27:5156–5169.

Zhang JF, Huang ZR, Tumati S, Northoff G (2020) Rest-task modulation of fMRI-derived global signal topography is mediated by transient coactivation patterns. PLoS Biology. 18:e3000733.

Conclusion

Connecting brain and psyche – project for a spatiotemporal neuroscience

"Project for a spatiotemporal neuroscience" I – complementing and extending Freud

Having provided empirical support for spatiotemporal neuroscience, we are now ready to provide an answer to Freud's original quest for an intimate link of psyche and brain as developed in his "project for a scientific psychology". Following Freud's view of the psyche, spatiotemporal neuroscience considers the brain's neural activity as topographic, dynamic, and essentially spatiotemporal. Hence, spatial-topographic and temporal-dynamic features provide the features that are shared by the brain's neural activity and the psyche's psychodynamic features, their "common currency". Taken in a nutshell, spatiotemporal neuroscience provides the missing link of brain and psyche, which remained elusive to Freud in his time. We therefore speak of the need for a "project for a spatiotemporal neuroscience".

What do we mean by "project for a spatiotemporal neuroscience", and how does it stand in relation to Freud's original "project for a scientific psychology"? The "project for a spatiotemporal neuroscience" aims to develop the kind of neuroscience that, by establishing a temporal-dynamic and spatial-topographic view of the brain and its various functions, allows for their intimate connection with the psyche's psychodynamic features. This complements and extends Freud's original project, which, due to the lack of neuroscientific research at its time, could not conceive the dynamic and topography

DOI: 10.4324/9781003132905-9

of the brain. Accordingly, the "project for a spatiotemporal neuro-science" provides Freud with the kind of neuroscience that allows him to intimately link his view of the psyche to the brain and thus to complement his original project.

"Project for a spatiotemporal neuroscience" II – empirical convergence with Solms' "(new) project for a scientific psychology"

How does our "project for a spatiotemporal neuroscience" stand in relation to the recently proposed "(new) project for a scientific psychology" by Mark Solms (2020)? Mark Solms recently pro-posed a "new scientific psychology" (2020, 2021) where he casts Freud's original "scientific psychology" in the terms of free energy and predictive coding. He uses the physical-biological framework of the free energy principle and predictive coding (PC) to account for psychodynamic concepts like memory, primary and secondary processes, cathexis, dreams, and the ego as basic structure or organi-zation. Following Freud's "scientific psychology", he uses the origi-nal text as template for reformulating it in terms of Friston's FEP coupled with the affective neuroscience by Panksepp.

How does Solms' project of a "new scientific psychology" stand in relation to the here proposed "project for a spatiotemporal neuro-science"? First and foremost, they are not exclusive but compatible. There is plenty of convergence between Friston's FEP coupled with PC on the one hand and the spatiotemporal approach to the brain in terms of spatiotemporal neuroscience. His "(new) project for a scientific psychology" thus converges with our "project for a spatio-temporal neuroscience".

Prediction and free energy are driven by a deeper layer of the brain's temporal dynamics, that is, deep temporal models (Friston et al. 2017; Kiebel et al. 2008) – spatiotemporal neuroscience may thus provide the temporal (and spatial-topographic) underpinnings driving PC, as we see in the case of the self. The same holds analo-gously in the case of FEP. The spatiotemporal, that is, dynamic and topographic, configurations in the matching of brain and environ-ment are key in mediating the degree of free energy, that is, FEP. Accordingly, both FEP and PC may be driven, on a holistic and thus deeper and more fundamental level, by dynamic and topography. Spatiotemporal neuroscience thus provides a deeper more holistic and comprehensive empirical layer of the brain that can integrate and make us better understand how the brain can yield PC and FEP. Hence, our "project for a spatiotemporal neuroscience" empirically converges with and complements Solms' "(new) project for a scientific psychology".

"Project for a spatiotemporal neuroscience" III – conceptual extension of Solms' "(new) project for a scientific psychology"

Do we need both FEP/PC and spatiotemporal neuroscience? Or is one sufficient to explain the psyche? FEP/PC explain and mathematically formulate brilliantly the physical-biological features of the brain, as both FEP and PC strongly borrow from physics and biology. However, that leaves open in both FEP/PC and Solms how the brain's states are connected to and, ultimately, can transform into psychical or mental states. Let us highlight this point.

We are encountering theoretical and empirical questions in our aim to intimately connect brain and psyche: what provides the necessary condition or intrinsic feature of the transition and connection from brain to psyche? Why and how does the brain's neural activity transform into psychic activity with its various functions (affective, social, cognitive, etc.) shaped by PC/FEP? Necessary connection (as theoretical concept) and transformation (as empirical concept) mean here that if the neuronal state appears in a particular way, it cannot avoid being associated with or entailing the presence of a particular psychical or mental state. We are thus encountering a "gap of contingency" between brain and psyche, something that, in the specific instance of consciousness, has also been described as a "hard problem" in philosophy (Chalmers 1996).

How can we close the "gap of contingency" between brain and psyche? This is the moment where spatiotemporal neuroscience, together with the assumption of "common currency", comes in. Brain and psyche share spatial-topographic and temporal-dynamic features as their "common currency" that underlie and shape PC and FEP and subsequently the respective affective and cognitive functions. This, as detailed in Northoff (2018), provides an intrinsic or necessary a posteriori connection of brain and psyche. The "gap of contingency" can consequently be closed and, even stronger, be resolved by spatiotemporal neuroscience through its assumption of spatial topography and temporal dynamic providing the "common currency" of brain and psyche.

This carries major implications for the relationship of our "project for a spatiotemporal neuroscience" to Solms' "(new) project for a scientific psychology". By providing analogous views of brain and psyche in terms of topography, dynamic, and spatiotemporality, the "project for a spatiotemporal neuroscience" bridges and resolves the "gap of contingency" of brain and psyche. Since the "gap of contingency" is still present in Friston's concepts of FEP and PC, Solms' "(new) project for a scientific psychology" cannot avoid this gap either.

This is the moment where the "(new) project for a scientific psychology" may want to turn to our "project for a spatiotemporal neuroscience": the latter's focus on the brain's topography and dynamic providing the shared feature or "common currency" with the psyche can close the "gap of contingency" in Solms' "(new) project for a scientific psychology". This gap is closed by providing the direct connection of neural and mental activity, that is, their transition or bridge where neural activity is transformed into mental activity – this was already foreseen by Carl Gustav Jung: "The brain might be a transformer station, in which the relatively infinite tension or intensity of the psyche proper is transformed into perceptible frequencies or 'extensions'" (1928). Taken in this sense, the "project for a spatiotemporal neuroscience" conceptually extends the "(new) project for a scientific psychology" by providing a more intimate, that is, necessary a posteriori (Northoff 2018), connection of brain and psyche.

Closing the "gap of contingency" of brain and psyche is not only of theoretical-conceptual importance but also in a very practical sense. The "project for a spatiotemporal neuroscience" allows us to develop a novel form of psychodynamic psychotherapy, namely spatiotemporal psychotherapy. Although it remains to be fully explicated, we at least want to provide some initial hints about such temporally and spatially based psychotherapy.

Practical relevance – do we need spatiotemporal psychotherapy?

Spatiotemporal psychotherapy I – spatial and temporal integration of the client's self through the therapist

What is the goal of psychotherapy? In our view, the goal of psychotherapy is (i) to reverse maladaptive topographic-dynamic reorganization of brain and (ii) to establish a more adaptive and stable spatiotemporal nestedness of brain and self, thereby re-establishing a proper nested hierarchy of self. This process, in accordance with contemporary psychoanalysis, might serve to re-establish the subjective sense of integrity, coherence, and continuity of self over time and space, similar to what has been described by Philip Bromberg: "health is the ability to stand in the spaces between realities without losing any of them – the capacity to feel like one self while being many" (1996, 166).

Psychotherapeutically, this means that we may need to operate at the subjects' level of perception (or experience) of time, that is, dynamics, and space, that is, topography, as the building blocks of individuals self-states (and ultimately their brain's temporal-dynamic and spatial-topographic structure) to remedy and heal their discrepancies, discontinuities, and dis-integrity of the sense of self. In this context we explicitly refer to contemporary psychoanalysis of self and relatedness (i.e., object relations), leaving beyond classical concepts of psychoanalysis such as drives, conflicts, and defense mechanisms. Our aim (and our target) is here to focus on the sense of self and its intrinsic features.

For instance, the therapist may need to operate on the building blocks of consciousness and unconscious processing through spatial-topographic and temporal-dynamic means: the therapist needs to connect (virtually or symbolically) her/his larger (spatial-topographic and temporal-dynamic) scales of her/his own exteroceptive and/or mental self to the client's more restricted interoceptive self. Pragmatically this means that operating in the dual relational field, the therapist must operate in the transferential-counter-transferential matrix using the "common currency" of time and space as the cardinal points to note and *work through* the moments of rupture of the sense of self and its intrinsic features.

This analytical dance in the transitional space and time of the real and the virtual relationship between the two subjects made by continuous "ruptures and repairs" provides the client with the opportunity to integrate and nest her/his own more restricted spatiotemporal scales of her/his interoceptive self in a virtual, that is, interpersonal, way into the larger ones of her/his therapist. That, in turn, will allow the client to process the traumatic input relationships in a non-threatening and non-disrupting way for her/his own self without becoming fragmented and losing the access to one's interoceptive self: the traumatic input relationships associated with the own interoceptive self are now integrated and nested virtually (or symbolically) within the therapists' larger spatiotemporal scales (of the therapist's exteroceptive and mental self).

Accordingly, the therapeutic aim here is to spatially and temporally reintegrate the different layers of self: that serves the purpose to connect the different layers of self such that they can become conscious together rather than being split off and isolated into the dynamic unconscious (as in dissociation). Dissociation here operates in terms of lack of integration between the different layers of the self (Scalabrini et al. 2020). Consequently, healing the self means to re-establish the sense of self-continuity beyond the dissociation of its trauma. This is possible by re-stablishing and/or reorganizing the topography and dynamic of the nested hierarchy of both self and its brain through spatial and temporal means – this amounts to what we here describe as "spatiotemporal psychotherapy".

Spatiotemporal psychotherapy II – timing, spatialness, dynamic and shared time-space

What is spatiotemporal psychotherapy? Spatiotemporal psychotherapy consists in modulating the individual's subjectively perceived (consciously and unconsciously) time- and space-scales on both neural and psychological levels. This process calls into account the role of the therapist that here works at the edges of different affective and self-states characterized by their respective time- and space-scales. The primary purpose of the therapist is to reach and integrate their clients' dissociated spatiotemporal layers of self with their respective affects and thoughts (this is consistent with the work on different traumatic levels that has been clinically described by Mucci 2013, 2018; Mucci and Scalabrini 2021).

The primary means of such spatiotemporal psychotherapy are thus spatial and temporal in both intra-personal experience/perception and inter-personal transference. This targets the most basic and fundamental layers of existence, the spatiotemporal coordinates that tie together different people like therapist and client while, at the same time, being most vulnerable to traumatic events and influences. Importantly, the main therapeutic direction of client–therapist interaction is from their shared inter-personal space and time to the intra-personal experiences/perceptions of the client (and those of the therapist).

How does spatiotemporal psychotherapy work? For instance, the therapist may provide more stable, regular, and continuous mixture of slow and fast time-scales trying to be "sufficiently" aligned with the patient in the analytic dance. This process aims to regularize, stabilize, and make the temporal dynamic flow of the client's neural and psychic activity more continuous, while, at the same time, allowing integrating temporal discontinuity and change as related to traumata. This, as we hypothesize, should complement and mirror the client's self-state, increasing these subjects' arousal level and modulating their affect and emotion as well as their thought dynamic. Hence, timing, spatialness, and temporal dynamic within the interaction of client and therapist will be key in such a psychotherapeutic regulatory approach.

A psychotherapy that is inter-personally attuned in time and aligned in space might provide a more comprehensive, basic, and extensive operating field that also embeds and contains affective, social, and cognitive functions within a larger more comprehensive context. Here we suggest therapists work using these spatiotemporal coordinates beyond the contents and narratives of the patients. The shared time and space between therapist and client might here be seen as an operating commonly shared interpersonal spatiotemporal field, which makes possible the reorganization and transformation of the client's intra-personal nested hierarchy of self through its spatiotemporal manifestation within her/his brain (see Spagnolo and Northoff 2021).

In case of very severe psychiatric patients, one could also complement such a temporo-spatial psychotherapy by biological intervention operating on the basis of the brain's spatiotemporal features. For instance, transcranial magnetic stimulation may, if stimulating in the "right" frequency, foster and facilitate slow–fast temporal integration on the neuronal level of, for instance, the default-mode network in order to help the client to remit from dissociating her/ his own mental self and to enlarge its spatial and temporal scales beyond those related to its "traumatic shrinking". That, in turn, provides the ground for the more virtual or symbolic work with the therapist to reorder, reintegrate, and renest the client's mental self within her/his own intero- and exteroceptive self.

References

Bromberg PM (1996) Standing in the spaces: The multiplicity of self and the psychoanalytic relationship. Cont. Psychoanalysis. 32:509–535. doi: 10.1080/00107530.1996.10746334

Chalmers D (1996) The conscious mind. Oxford University Press, Oxford.

Friston KJ, Rosch R, Parr T, Price C, Bowman H (2017) Deep temporal models and active inference. Neurosci Biobehav Rev. Jun;77:388–402. doi: 10.1016/j.neubiorev.2017.04.009. Epub 2017 Apr 14.

Jung C (1928) Letters, Vol. II, Pages 43–47.

Kiebel SJ, Daunizeau J, Friston KJ (2008) A hierarchy of time-scales and the brain. PLoS Comput Biol. 4(11):e1000209. doi: 10.1371/journal.pcbi.1000209

Mucci C (2013) Beyond individual and collective trauma: Intergenerational transmission, psychoanalytic treatment, and the dynamics of forgiveness. Routledge, Abingdon, UK.

Mucci C (2018) Borderline bodies: Affect regulation therapy for personality disorders (Norton Series on Interpersonal Neurobiology). WW Norton & Company, New York.

Mucci C, Scalabrini A (2021) Traumatic effects beyond diagnosis: The impact of dissociation on the mind-body-brain system. Psychoanal. Psychol. doi: 10.1037/pap0000332

Northoff G (2018) The spontaneous brain: From the mind-body to the world-brain problem. MIT Press, Cambridge, MA. doi: 10.7551/mitpress/9780262038072.001.0001

Scalabrini A, Mucci C, Esposito R, Damiani S, Northoff G (2020) Dissociation as a disorder of integration: On the footsteps of Pierre Janet.

Prog Neuropsychopharmacol Biol Psychiatry. Jul 13;101:109928. doi: 10.1016/j.pnpbp.2020.109928

Solms M (2020) New project for a scientific psychology: General scheme. Neuropsychoanalysis. 22:5–35. doi: 10.1080/15294145.2020.1833361

Solms M (2021) The hidden spring: A journey to the source of consciousness. WW Norton & Company, New York.

Spagnoli R, Northoff G (2021) The dynamic self. Routledge, London, New York.

Index